D0420470

20-00

DEVELOPING HR TALENT

Developing HR Talent

Building a Strategic Partnership with the Business

Kirsty Saddler and Jan Hills

GOWER

© Kirsty Saddler and Jan Hills 2011

All rights reserved. No part of this publication may be reproduced, stored in a retrieval system or transmitted in any form or by any means, electronic, mechanical, photocopying, recording or otherwise without the prior permission of the publisher.

Kirsty Saddler and Jan Hills have asserted their moral rights under the Copyright, Designs and Patents Act, 1988, to be identified as the authors of this work.

Published by
Gower Publishing Limited
Wey Court East
Union Road
Farnham
Surrey GU9 7PT
England

Gower Publishing Company
Suite 420
101 Cherry Street
Burlington, VT 05401-4405
USA

www.gowerpublishing.com

British Library Cataloguing in Publication Data
Saddler, Kirsty.
  Developing HR talent : building a strategic partnership
  with the business. -- (The Gower HR transformation series)
  1. Personnel management--Practice.
  I. Title II. Series III. Hills, Jan.
  658.3-dc22

  ISBN: 978-0-566-08829-2 (pbk)
  ISBN: 978-0-7546-8167-0 (ebk)

Library of Congress Cataloging-in-Publication Data
Saddler, Kirsty.
  Developing HR talent : building a strategic partnership with the business / Kirsty Saddler and Jan Hills.
    p. cm. -- (The Gower HR transformation series)
  Includes index.
  ISBN 978-0-566-08829-2 (pbk.) -- ISBN 978-0-7546-8167-0
  (ebook) 1. Personnel management. 2. Manpower planning. 3. Strategic planning. I. Hills, Jan. II. Title.
  HF5549.S122 2010
  658.3'14--dc22
                                                        2010025551

MIX
Paper from
responsible sources
FSC
www.fsc.org   FSC® C018575

Printed and bound in Great Britain by the
MPG Books Group, UK

658. 311
SAD
131486

NNR 13

LIBRARY

Contents

List of Figures

Summary of the Contents

INTRODUCTION

In this chapter we summarise the requirement for HR to transform, what this means in structural terms; the skills needed to support this new model and therefore the new pressure this brings to bear on HR to manage, develop and retain its talent.

CHAPTER 1: HR TALENT MANAGEMENT

We describe some of the issues associated with talent management in the HR function and how historical attitudes are hampering the function in realising its full potential. HR people are experts in developing others potential within the business, yet this seems to have discouraged rather than encouraged the majority of HR Directors (HRDs) to use this expertise in their own function. We frequently find that HR is the hardest to convince that there is a need to provide development and a new approach to career management if they are to fully perform.

CHAPTER 2: THE SKILLS AND MINDSET FOR SUCCESS

With 81 per cent of medium to large companies having completed, undertaking or about to start major HR transformation (CIPD Report, *Strategic HR Contribution*, 2007) the focus is now on the long-term success of these restructures; ensuring that the promised added strategic value to the business becomes a reality. We examine what skills and mindset are needed to ensure that HR can truly partner the business. We summarise our research in this area and the implications.

CHAPTER 3: TALENT MANAGEMENT – BEST PRACTICE FOR HR

There are organisations leading the way in HR development, with innovative approaches. Orion has developed a model for successful HR development. We share our model and examples, and describe best practice in talent management for HR.

CHAPTER 4: DEVELOPING YOUR HR FUNCTION

Talent management is top of the agenda for many organisations and an area where HR have focused their efforts. However, these skills and innovations are not consistently applied. Frequently, even when there is a focus on identifying HR talent, this is not translated into a development programme across the function.

CHAPTER 5: CAREER MANAGEMENT

Based on the findings from our research *'Facing up to the Future'* (available from www.orion-partners.com) we share approaches to career management in the transformed HR function, the lessons learnt and successful practice from organisations who took part in the research. We look at the demands of the new multi-career paths of HR and how to address these challenges. We also look at the best use of the new flatter organisational structure and the opportunities it creates for more diverse careers.

CHAPTER 6: ATTRACTING THE RIGHT TALENT

Talent management is not just about developing those already in the function. Attracting people from outside of the function can be a source of new blood and stimulate performance within HR. We discuss some of the ideas that are working in this area.

CHAPTER 7: ACHIEVING A RETURN FROM YOUR DEVELOPMENT INVESTMENT

It is essential that your investment in developing HR can be justified through beneficial behavioural changes and the value returned to the business. Good development will also improve retention and motivation. We examine some practical methods you can implement to ensure that development sticks and becomes embedded in day-to-day work behaviours that have a long lasting benefit to the business.

CHAPTER 8: CONCLUSION

Here we summarise our ten top lessons learnt from working with organisations that are focusing on developing their HR function.

Introduction

The HR function has been preoccupied with moving into a strategic role with the business since the late 1990s. In 2007 the CIPD Report, *The Changing HR Function*, found that 53 per cent of organisations researched had restructured their HR function in the previous year and that 81 per cent had done so over the prior 5 years. This transformed HR model, while often described in structural terms, is about creating a function that has the skills and mindset to partner with the business to formulate and execute strategy. This puts demands on HRDs to equip their function in a way that was never required in the past.

The transformed model divides HR into three areas of responsibility and focus. These areas are:

- *Shared Service Centres* (SSC) that carry out the routine, administrative and transactional aspects of HR. The SSC creates economies of scale and depth of expertise in what has been described as 'the service delivery function' within HR.

- *Centres of Expertise or Excellence* (CoE), responsible for process, policy and company-wide strategic initiatives. The disciplines covered here vary by company, but will typically include learning and development, compensation, employee relations and recruitment.

- *HR Business Partners* (HRBPs) focus on working closely with the business or business unit on the formation and execution of strategy as part of the management team.

This separation of responsibility and focus on strategic contribution has created demands on HR to develop new skills. These skills range from deeper expertise in operational and technology-type disciplines to a greater involvement and understanding of the business as well as a more commercial and analytical approach.

Even for organisations that have not adopted the transformed HR model, the expectations on HR and the skills needed to address those expectations mean that developing new skills still sits squarely on the HR agenda.

All these changes mean that the talent pool within HR can no longer be defined as before. The talent profile has irreversibly changed, as must the approach to developing it. This book will guide you through the new skills and changes to talent and career management required in the transformed model. It will point you to potential solutions and good practice, which has worked for other companies.

① HR Talent Management

THE LEGACY OF THE PAST

The importance of talent management and development in achieving superior business results is generally accepted. US companies listed as the highest rated Fortune 100 firms to work for, outperform others by creating a return on investment of 14 per cent compared to 6 per cent for those not listed (Professor Alex Edmans at Wharton, *Does the Stock Market Fully Value intangibles? Employee Satisfaction and Equity Prices*, June 2008). Edmans admits that his study cannot isolate the factor that creates this increased return. Whether it is down to employee satisfaction alone or good management that creates that employee satisfaction is an unknown. But he points out that this does not really matter. This external measure of employee satisfaction is a guide to the importance of intangibles. The inclusion on the Fortune list should be an indicator to investors of the quality of the return they can expect from the firm. But it is the trend that this research points to that should be of most interest to HR people.

Overall, Edmans' research is part of a broader shift among academics to develop new theories focused on the modern firm. 'When I was at Morgan Stanley, we would value firms according to their tangible assets, cash flows and earnings – which are common across most of Wall Street and much existing academic research,' Edmans says. 'But nowadays, significant components of a firm's value cannot be captured by accounting numbers.' Given most intangibles fall into HR's remit this is an opportunity for HR to demonstrate and measure the value they add to achieving business goals. To be effective at this HR need to have the skills and mindset to impact the intangibles, such as culture, employee engagement and leadership.

The value and importance of talent management across the business is agreed. It is extraordinary then to recognise that in the clamour to win the war for talent, HR has neglected to focus on talent managing its own function. The value of developing HR staff as a driver to improve strategic contribution is only now becoming a serious discussion topic. Research by the Corporate Leadership Council (CLC) (Chief Human Resources Officer Survey, CLC, 2006) found that only 30 per cent of HRDs applied talent management disciplines to their own function.

As expressed by the global HRD of a major financial institution:

> *The HR function has been under so much pressure in the past 15 years to evolve as a strategic business partner and address what has been commonly touted as the 'global war for talent' that it almost forgot to focus on itself and its own need for a talent pipeline.*

With the change from an HR functional structure to the model of HRBPs, CoE and SSC, the associated shift in focus for each area has outmoded traditional approaches to attracting, developing and retaining talent.

However, there is more to it than the issues created by HR's changing structure. When we think about HR talent development we raise some thorny issues about the HR function in general. HR as a function exhibits some tendencies that plague its view of itself. In a survey of Chief Human Resource Officers, CLC (*Defining the Critical Skills of HR Staff*, 2006) HR functions rated themselves best at applying methods that involved recruiting new staff, 41 per cent of organisations rated themselves as effective at this. However, the survey showed only one in four effectively developed existing HR staff.

One issue for HR is a tendency to be inward looking and self-conscious about how HR adds value to the business. This has been prevalent since the mid-1990s, when Ulrich (David Ulrich, *Human Resource Champions*) began to push HR into a more strategic role. Amazingly, we still come across people in the function arguing that this is not a legitimate role for HR and that the business does not want to work with HR in a strategic manner. This debate has led to HR, in our view, being overly inward looking, focused more on itself than the business. Which leads to a self-fulfilling prophesy; too much self focus leads to a lack of added value and questions from the business about HR's value.

HR also has a tendency to deny itself the same budget and levels of access to development as the rest of the organisation. It is not uncommon to hear HRDs say that their function does not take part in development programmes as 'they are for the business', as if HR is somehow not part of the same organisation. HR also expresses its inferiority complex by translating the need for broader development into an admission of inherent weakness. This has resulted in a lack of budget and passion for the right kind of development. The focus has mainly been on technical skills with limited development in the areas of business and interpersonal skills. We are, however, starting to see a shift with a broad recognition that if HR is going to 'business partner', it needs the same level of development opportunities as the people it is partnering with.

A particular issue that has contributed to HR's difficulties is their tendency to focus on transforming the structure and IT capability of the function at the expense of the capabilities and mindset. Our own survey of HR people found that while many had made some transformation, not all had included all the elements (see Figure 1.1).

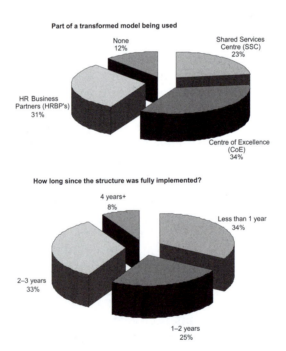

Figure 1.1   Orion Partners survey from our website, October 2008

While the motivation for making change was primarily adding value to the business other factors were also important including making a more strategic contribution. The demands that drove these changes were rated as shown in the graphs below (see Figures 1.2).

Figure 1.2   Demands driving changes in HR practice

7

The emphasis in the survey on achieving better service and a more strategic contribution, rather than just on cost and efficiency, points to the need for a change in capability across HR; not just structural change.

THE NEW GLASS CEILING

The transformed HR structures frequently create a large gap between SSCs, CoEs and HRBPs roles. There are now few, if any roles, which will develop the next generation of HRBPs from the other areas. Our research on career paths (*Facing up to the Future*) consistently found that those in early career roles with ambitions to develop are struggling to move on from the SSC roles and are hitting a glass ceiling; clearly a major de-motivator.

The research identified that some of the key skills required for HRBPs, such as relationship management and business understanding, are not developed in the SSC. Shared Service Centres roles prove challenging when early career HR professionals need to get a good business understanding and develop a sense of 'what will work' in the organisation. As a result organisations are losing candidates at early points in their career as they seek generalist experience in smaller organisations with more traditional HR functions to allow them to break out of SSC roles. Conversely, the emphasis on the HRBP job is distracting people at earlier career levels from taking the roles that will move them into the range of HR jobs – no other role seems to matter.

Our senior level participants, who reflected on how early 'coalface' experience was critical to moving on, identified examples of this. The most common route was through employee relations roles. Surprisingly these roles were not valued for the HR technical knowledge provided, but rather because they built understanding of the business, while establishing credibility and empathy with business managers. All of these, in more sophisticated forms, are key skills for an HRBP. This is a very interesting point; an aspect of HR that appears to be undervalued generally is a very useful source of experience for developing skills and mindset for the transformed HR function:

> *The HR employee relations role is about really knowing the business and its people, it is about understanding the shop floor and making an impact in that environment. My training ground for that was dealing with conflict between people as part of my first role as a graduate trainee. We are not creating enough opportunities for our people to learn that now.*
>
> *HR Director, professional services firm*

The research examined the impact this is having on those moving out of their first roles. HR recruiters, Digby Morgan, provided their observations:

> *There is a shortage of good business candidates with a depth and breadth of HR knowledge and who are good communicators and relationship builders. Their most successful candidates are those who have built a broad base of skills before specialising, these candidates tend to come from smaller organisations.*
>
> *In smaller companies, while the Business Partner, Shared Service and Centre of Expertise model may not be in place, candidates have been exposed to a broader*

range of HR activity. Candidates in larger organisations have typically had more structured early careers, but do not often show the breadth of skills needed to move on, with many coming from narrow shared service backgrounds. These candidates are finding that they have to move organisations to obtain the breadth they need to move on in their HR careers.

Director, Digby Morgan

Few organisations have carefully thought through how to develop key HRBP skills as part of their implementation of new HR services. However, as we have seen, many are now rethinking HR structures and development programmes as a result of pressure to build internal HR talent.

EXTERNAL RECRUITMENT

As HR has evolved, its employee value proposition has not kept pace and now lacks focus and definition. There is a wide disparity between the drivers that attract top talent to HR compared to other disciplines, such as finance, strategy, marketing and sales. The disparity primarily centres on HR's kudos, compensation and career opportunities.

Despite HR leaders and Chief Executive Officers (CEOs) focusing on the need to transform HR, there continues to be a limiting belief associated with the value that HR adds to the business and its overall effectiveness. Two-thirds of line managers are reported to perceive HR's effectiveness in creating business value to be neutral or ineffective; there is an associated issue in that this perception compounds the difficulty of encouraging managers from the line to join

HR (SHRM seen as necessary evil. *Management Issues*, 9 May 2008).

The second factor is to do with career advancement, both within HR and as a stepping stone to the most senior company roles. We are seeing more HRDs reaching board level, but very few, if any, are becoming CEOs. In addition, few high potential employees in other disciplines would currently consider a stint in HR as career enhancing. Going forward, it is possible that as HR builds its strategic business credentials it will become as recognised as a key stepping stone in developing general business executives as an assignment in finance, operations or sales. This development component is integral to building these next generation HR career paths. HR must recognise its unique opportunity as purveyors of talent to the business. HR assignments must be part of the general talent development proposition for business leadership roles:

> *Running a business is about process and people leadership. Our HR person had both. That's why she's now running one of our problem businesses that needs to be turned around.*
>
> *CEO, European financial services business*

② The Skills and Mindset for Success

Different skills and beliefs are needed to fulfil the new roles being created across HR. To be successful in these roles the importance of underlying beliefs, values and a sense of purpose are now being recognised.

There are three important elements to consider in relation to these new roles:

The person – the skills, background and development experiences that HR professionals must have.

Job design – the accountability of individual HR professionals and the interactions they have with the business and other members of the HR function and the boundaries between roles.

HR's structure and budget – HR's structure, budget, technology and design are recognised as enablers for HR.

Research indicates that the strategic impact of the HRBP role makes the most significant contribution to the return on investment for the business (*Building Next Generation HR Line*

Partnerships. Preview of research findings, CLC, 2007). It is, therefore, reasonable to focus on the HRBP role's strategic development as a priority. Of the three factors: (1) the person; (2) job design; and (3) HR's structure, CLC's research concludes that job design is the most important factor affecting HR's ability to provide strategic support. While the person, including background, skill set and development experiences, makes the most significant impact on an individual's success within the profession.

HR leaders are placing more emphasis on identifying what it takes for HR professionals to become exceptional. But there are still many theories and different points of view. Most HR functions have their own competency model. What are the exact skills and development experiences required to enable individuals to deliver maximum impact to the business?

There have been many attempts to define what makes HR people successful. Until recently there has not been a dedicated study that concentrates on isolating the differentiating factors between the very best and an average HRBP. Orion Partners has filled this gap through research focusing primarily on the HRBP role. By 2004, we found that too many client organisations were struggling with the answer to that question. This was hampering clients' ability to identify the best candidates, guide and develop those already in position and consequently to deliver the full value of the HR transformation to the business clients.

Orion Partners decided to invest in a search for some answers by conducting a global study using a modelling technique it developed called the 'Success Profile'.

HOW THE STUDY WAS CONDUCTED

SELECTING THE BUSINESS PARTNERS

The study began with a group of 30 HRBPs from a range of industries across both the public and private sector.

The qualifying criteria for inclusion were that they:

- Were identified by their business line clients as making an exceptional strategic contribution to the business.

- Had at least 10 years experience in HR.

- Had full responsibility for delivering the HR agenda for their organisation, region or part of the business.

- Were in a role where the transactional aspects were being delivered by others.

They were located in the UK, USA, Europe and Asia, and had varying geographic remits; global, regional and local.

GATHERING THE DATA

Participants were interviewed in-depth using a structured format that elicited information about instances when they had been exceptionally successful in their role and times when they had been less successful.

In each case the interview drilled down into detail about their experiences at five levels:

1. *When and where* – the circumstantial environment in which the event occurred.

2. *What* – the actions they took; what they did.

3. *How* – the capabilities they drew on; how they decided on actions.

4. *Why* – the beliefs and values that drove their decisions and led to their actions.

5. *Who* – their sense of identity and purpose in the situation; who they are in their role.

While the methodology is similar to that used in developing competency frameworks, it is important to note that the deeper dimensions focused on in the 'Success Profile' (the how, why and who) produced a much richer picture of the full conditions that generate success.

THE ANALYSIS

The data was analysed by searching for the consistent patterns within each individual's experience (their personal blueprint for success) and subsequently between participants across the population (their shared blueprint for success). The patterns identified for individuals and across the group were the presence or absence of an element in a number of successful incidents or the presence, or absence, of an element in unsuccessful incidents.

This study highlighted that while common skill gaps and development needs in traditional HR roles were understood

SELF-BELIEF

The business partners we interviewed believed deeply in the function and its value to the strategic agenda of the business. They saw themselves as equal partners with the business managers in driving success through the people agenda. They consistently defined their purpose in terms of their contribution to strategy and business performance.

Beyond these deeply supportive beliefs about the importance of what they do, the best HRBPs also had profound confidence in their own skills and their ability to use them to make the right things happen in the business.

Sample quotes on self-belief:

> *'My values guide my decisions in the context of the culture and business goals.'*

> *'I have a strong internal compass that guides my actions.'*

> *'I believe that HR makes as much difference to the success of the business as any function.'*

> *'I believe I have the skills and knowledge to make a difference in the business.'*

> *'I believe I am equal to others in the management team.'*

> *'It is impossible to convince the client of something you don't believe in.'*

INDEPENDENCE

Every one of the participants in our study described willingness, or even in some cases an obligation, to have an independent point of view. Having an opinion alone, however, is not enough. Participants also consistently described the need to have the courage to express their point of view even at the risk of being unpopular. In addition, they described the need for persistence in maintaining their position in the face of opposition.

They frequently described this ability to have and hold on to an independent opinion as one of the attributes most likely to earn the respect of their clients and enable them to build the depth of relationship required to be powerfully influential.

Sample quotes on independence:

> 'Sometimes you have to take a risk.'

> 'I've never been afraid of being fired for expressing my opinion.'

> 'To be an objective third party who knows the business.'

> 'Be true to yourself.'

> 'It's my job to raise the un-discussable.'

> 'Be willing to be tested.'

> 'Clients value honesty and candour.'

*'Holding up the mirror and challenging assumptions
is critical for success.'*

BUSINESS ACUMEN

The participants in our study could articulate and understand
the strategy and the key drivers of success. They had a focus
on the competition and deep understanding of their industry
or sector. They knew how their piece of the business interfaced
with the rest of the organisation.

They consistently mentioned the need to think and
communicate in business terms and to focus on business
outcomes and results, not on HR processes and jargon.

This way of thinking and communicating was seen as the
second powerful contributor to earning the respect of clients.

Sample quotes on business acumen:

*'Articulate the business strategy and the HR (people
and structure) implications.'*

*'Make links across the business – take a holistic
view.'*

*'Have a broad interest and knowledge, not just HR but
economic and political implications.'*

'Use the business language.'

'What is the conversation going to sound like?'

'Focus on business outcomes – that is what strategy is.'

'Developing a deep understanding of the client builds the relationship and the knowledge of how to position ideas.'

'Position ideas so the business understands the benefits.'

RELATIONSHIPS

The group we studied constantly referred to the importance of their relationships and described how they invested heavily in building strength, depth and trust in their relations with others. They did not focus on client relationships alone, but recognised the need for equally strong relationships with colleagues across the HR function. What was also striking about these relationships was that they were not always comfortable, but real, honest and often challenging.

Time and time again they described having been able to make a difference and get things done as a direct result of the strength of their relationships.

Sample quotes on relationships:

'Build trusting relationships for the purpose of improving the effectiveness of people.'

'Listen to the words, tone and emotions.'

'Create opportunities to interact.'

'Put yourself in the client's shoes.'

'Know the client's interest, concerns and values.'

'Be conscious of the implicit message.'

'It is imperative to work with people.'

'Relationships are built over time and multiple transactions.'

'I will challenge the client where their actions will damage the business or themselves.'

BUSINESS RESULTS DELIVERY

Our HRBPs shared a common focus on delivering quality business outcomes. They had fully embraced the change within their function and held themselves accountable for delivering results through others within HR. They took responsibility for influencing the corporate HR agenda to meet the needs of their clients, but also took responsibility for educating their clients about the importance of the corporate HR agenda. They were strong role models for their teams to follow.

A strong track record of delivering the right results for the business was the other factor in earning the respect and trust of the business clients.

Sample quotes on business results delivery:

'Deliver the whole HR function.'

'My mindset is I'm accountable but not responsible for the delivery.'

'Structure support to free up resource for the strategic agenda.'

'Influence the corporate agenda.'

'Help the line manager access the function.'

'Educate the client.'

'HR interventions (and products) must align with business goals and reinforce each other.'

'There are many solutions to any business issue. It is important to be flexible and to find a solution that the client can buy-in to.'

'Set standards and model them.'

At its heart, the HRBPs role is about the right mindset (see Figure 2.2).

Figure 2.2   The HR results triangle

THE NEW TECHNICAL SKILLS

The separation of responsibility across HR and the focus on strategic contribution has created demands to develop new skills.

Traditionally HR has focused on the technical skills associated with the employee life cycle. Hiring, compensating, managing performance and leaving the organisation. In the transformed HR structure additional skills are needed.

For people in shared services – this is about managing slick processes, continually improving the administrative and transactional work, and the customer experience. Much of this technical expertise is about customer relations, process management and maximising resources while ensuring that employees are engaged.

For people in centres of expertise – it is about deep technical expertise in their specialism. However, it is also about process re-engineering; making processes fit for purpose and adaptable enough to meet changing business needs and economic conditions.

For HRBPs – the emphasis is on keeping up to date with the employee life cycle tools while learning new technical skills: such as leading and managing change; work force planning; organisation design and development; and coaching and consulting. One HRD described the HRBP as needing the skills of a general practitioner doctor:

> *they need to know enough about each of the areas of HR technical competence – they must be able to analysis and diagnose the problem or opportunity for the business and to know when they need to refer the issue or opportunity to a specialist [Centres of Expertise or Excellence (CoE) person] or judge that they can handle the initiative successfully themselves.*

We see demands being made on HR to understand and be able to advise on change, organisation design and leadership development. There is still a way to go before the majority of HR people have a practical understanding of these areas and the confidence to adapt that understanding to their specific business situation. We also see too much theory and not enough practical advice. These new technical HR skills are every bit as important as understanding pensions, the law and recruitment practices, and it has implications on HR development too. HR teams, especially those in CoE and HRBP roles, need development and, most importantly, practical experience in change and organisational design.

So while new skills are an essential part of the picture, trying to address them in isolation from the person embodying them and that person's ability to relate to, influence and lead others will fail to create the best results possible.

Our work with organisations has shown that the skills and mindset needed by HRBPs are also important to the other areas of HR. Organisations lose out on some potential in their transformation if they do not equip their SSC and CoE managers, as well as their HRBPs to be able to:

- have the confidence to stand up for what is right;

- believe deeply in the value of what they do;

- think, talk and act strategically;

- know the business as well as the line does;

- develop strong client relationships;

- influence and lead others;

- understand the whole HR picture and how to deliver it to clients;

- work effectively with HR colleagues;

- coach, consult and contract effectively;

- monitor, measure and understand results.

THE IMPLICATIONS

What is clear from these findings is that it is not enough for an HRBP to have strong HR skills and knowledge. These may be necessary, but they are essentially baseline qualifying criteria. In selecting HRBPs, for the 'difference that makes the difference', companies must look deeper. In developing these skills they need to move away from transitional training methods. They must look for:

- Those who believe they deserve and can make good use of a seat at the management table, acting with independence and courage.

- Those who think, act and communicate like business people with real commercial instinct and knowledge.

- Those who are willing to invest in building strong, equal and challenging relationships with their clients and colleagues.

- Those who drive for the delivery of meaningful results for the business and can inspire their HR colleagues to join them in that drive.

- Those who see continuous development of their skills and mastery of applying these to the business context.

This can be a tall order and few high performing HRBPs are born with these skills and this mindset. These can be developed, but if they are to be developed successfully, the focus should be on the underlying beliefs of the HRBP; their ways of thinking about and approaching what they do. Skills alone will not generate exceptional success.

Since the completion of the original study, we have added to our database by interviewing many HRBPs in our client organisations. The database now stands at over 100 and the findings have been consistent between the original study and the larger group.

③ Talent Management – Best Practice for HR

Most HR departments are involved in a talent management project of some kind. Talent management is an area that has caught people's interest and particularly so now. Despite this ongoing activity, most companies remain concerned about the quality and quantity of their HR talent. We began to wonder why this was when there are so many companies running talent management projects:

> *The responsibility for finding a solution lies at HR's door and the main reason companies still lack the talent they need is because HR is not yet able to balance the different activities that talent management requires.*
>
> *HRD, financial service organisation*

Talent management processes usually begin with an analysis phase. The analysis identifies who has potential, who will succeed whom, and what talent is needed or missing from across

HR. For this phase to be successful, you need good analytical tools and a clear idea of what you are looking for. Most HR teams seem to have a good grasp of how to conduct effective analysis. There are detailed competency models in place and a process for determining who meets those competencies either formally through assessment or development centres, or more informally through input from line managers. Most companies also have a means of calibrating the opinions and rating of people across the function through a talent committee or similar. But talent management is not just about knowing who has potential.

There is a danger of spending too much time on the analysis stage and failing to progress sufficiently quickly to the next phase. This may well be because the initial analysis is tangible and naturally lends itself to presentations and reports demonstrating progress and activity. However, analysis alone does not complete the talent management process. A second phase is needed in order to develop the identified talent.

FOCUSING ON DEVELOPMENT

The second phase is designed to ensure that HR people have the experience and training needed to achieve their potential. It is during this phase that the process usually falls down. Why does development often receive less focus? We believe there are two main reasons.

First, developing a person's skills and talent is not a clear and linear process; different people require different types of assistance and they develop at different rates. Many HR functions struggle with the sheer complexity of this process. There is no catch-all programme that is suitable for everyone and that can be put into place quickly and then left to run its course. Rather, development is an opportunistic process that relies on watching and waiting to see how an individual responds and develops as a result of the training programme or business experience. This demands a flexible programme; and one that does not necessarily produce tidy numbers and statistics that lend themselves to a report.

Second, it is often unclear who has accountability for managing development. Many companies see it as the line manager's responsibility to facilitate the development process, but there is often little incentive for line managers to take this on and development is given low priority over the demands of the day job. HR managers often feel that if they develop their team's skills, the net result for them is that their team members will be promoted and they are left with a gap to fill. The HRD needs to focus on ways to incentivise line HR managers to develop their teams proactively.

For example, if SSC management develop a great team they themselves should get a bonus or promotion. Alternatively, line HR managers can be assigned more challenging tasks that will develop them and their people. Thus the manager keeps their people, rather than losing them to training days and also benefits as the team strengthens.

There are a number of skills needed in HR today that are common across different roles (see Figure 3.1). Talent management programmes need to focus on what is common to all as well as what are the specific needs of the individual.

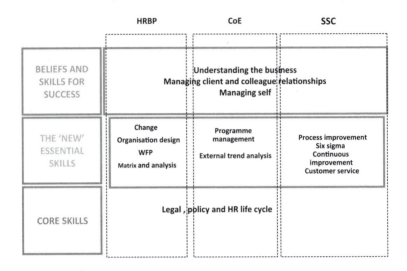

Figure 3.1 **HR skills shared commonly across the function**

IDENTIFYING SKILLS, POTENTIAL AND DEVELOPMENT NEEDS

One key aspect of career development in HR involves helping both the organisation and the individual to identify their talents and preferences across the different career options. There are several ways of doing this from 'training needs analysis' to 'assessment and development centres', which can offer a powerful vehicle for this process. We will look at each of these in a little more detail.

TRAINING NEEDS ANALYSIS

A training needs analysis is a way of surveying the training required and what's more, can help prioritise different areas of training that are needed by analysing the business and HR goals, and the skills required to meet those goals.

Most training analysis focuses on what people *aren't* doing and what they *aren't* skilled at. This might seem the obvious way to approach the issue of training – identify what people cannot do and work from there.

However, if the training analysis focuses only on what people are failing to do, it means that they are only approaching the training from a 'problem' frame of mind. By conducting the training analysis in this way, the subsequent training programme can only focus on those failed areas and fill in the skill gaps. This can undoubtedly be useful, but by only focusing on existing problems, the training needs analysis fails to identify any desired future outcomes.

Focusing on the negative will result in only remedial training. By asking people what they can not do and what they are not skilled at, the individual and the team can only progress so far. This means that the training focuses on those who are perhaps not doing so well, 'catching up' with how the best of the team already performs, rather than looking to where you would like that whole team to be. Looking at the training this way means that you are always looking backward rather than forward.

DIFFERENT RESULTS

By changing the focus of the training needs analysis to a positive approach, you immediately get different results that focus on what people are already doing well and how that can be developed further. Some of you may be concerned that this means that the people at the top move higher, leaving the people doing less well behind. We believe that this kind of training analysis can help to develop the whole team further.

At Orion Partners we use the 'Success Profile' as a tool to identify the most successful people within an HR team and to identify the working practices that they use to achieve that success. We have found that every company has its strengths and areas of success, but in most cases that success is not consistent across all areas of the function and for all people.

Our approach is to look at individuals and identify the five or six critical beliefs and working practices that make the highest achievers successful. One thing that we often find is that a number of high achievers who have taken part in the 'Success Profile' feel they would benefit from deeper training, so it has the double benefit of identifying how those high achievers can improve and continue to be challenged. Also those 'average' performers can be trained to adopt the successful practices of the high performers.

Training should be available for those that are already doing well, as much as those who have areas of difficulty. We find that many HR development programmes are seen as a way of fixing problems, but what they should be doing is advancing and aiding everyone to do much better. By refocusing the training needs analysis in this way, you are able to develop programmes that focus on successful practices, ensure everyone adopts these practices and help those who are already top performers achieve mastery.

STRUCTURE THE TRAINING

High achievers do not always know or understand what it is they do that makes them successful. By structuring the training to identify what employees are already doing well, it can be developed to expand on those successful working practices and beliefs. It can also provide people with alternative good practices so they have more flexibility in their working approach. By training people working at the top of their game, good practices will feed down to other members of the team.

So, what practical methods can you employ to make sure you invest in all of the team, including the high achievers? One easy way to begin to shift the focus of the training begins with the training analysis. When conducting interviews or surveys with senior HR managers to determine training needs, rather than asking: 'What does this group of SSC professionals need to be better at?'

Change the focus of the question to: 'What do your most successful people do that your average people don't?'

By refocusing the training needs analysis to look forward to desired outcomes, rather than only looking backwards and filling skills gaps, you can develop a training programme that can benefit the whole team.

ASSESSMENT AND DEVELOPMENT CENTRES

A well-established means of identifying development needs across the HR group are assessment and development centres. These have been around since the 1920s, first used in the German, USA and UK military to improve their officer selection processes. They have been growing in popularity in the corporate world globally since the 1950s and are now in widespread use across both the public and private sectors. The two types of centre, *assessment* or *development* have different intentions and as a starting point you need to identify which is more appropriate for your needs (see Figure 3.2).

ASSESSMENT VERSUS DEVELOPMENT

Much has been written on the differences between assessment centres and development centres, which are seen by some to be very significant. In our experience, the two types of centre are not as far apart in practice as is imagined.

It is rare, these days, to find assessment centres that do not contain a degree of development and virtually all development

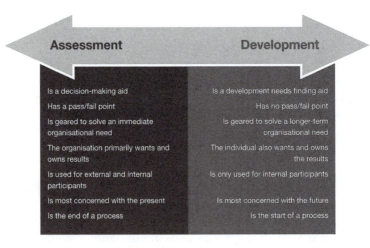

Assessment	Development
Is a decision-making aid	Is a development needs finding aid
Has a pass/fail point	Has no pass/fail point
Is geared to solve an immediate organisational need	Is geared to solve a longer-term organisational need
The organisation primarily wants and owns results	The individual also wants and owns the results
Is used for external and internal participants	Is only used for internal participants
Is most concerned with the present	Is most concerned with the future
Is the end of a process	Is the start of a process

Figure 3.2   The   elements   of   assessment   and development centres

centres, by their very nature, contain more than a degree of assessment. In reality, most centres sit somewhere on a spectrum between the two extremes and, while it is possible to describe clear differences at the ends, the middle ground is not black and white. The critically important point here is not so much to draw lines between the two to divide one from the other, but to be absolutely transparent about the intent of each particular centre and the uses to which data emerging from it will be put.

Mis-statement or confusion on this will lead, at best, to resentment and loss of respect for the sponsors among participants. At worst it can lead to resignations or legal action. If the results from the centre will be used to inform decisions on participant's current or future career, employment status or reward, the intent is assessment and should be clearly named as such.

WHY AND WHEN TO USE THEM

Well designed and run assessment and development centres are extremely useful tools in HR transformation. Their benefits include the fact that they:

- Provide more robust and objective results than other processes.

- Provide a greater depth and granularity of data and insight than other processes.

- Are seen to be fair and thorough.

- Give participants the opportunity to have a realistic experience of being in the new role, ahead of actually having to do it.

- Allow clear comparisons to be made across whole groups.

- Can be measured for predictive validity over time.

There are some situations in which they can be particularly valuable, for example:

SELECTION

In a situation when candidates need to be assessed on their suitability for a role, for example: single vacancy; multiple vacancies; promotions; restructuring; or transformation.

TALENT MANAGEMENT

They can help in defining and developing high potential and fast track populations. More generally, they are useful for career development in helping to determine the needs and potential of individuals at all levels. They deliver consistency and tend to give individuals greater ownership of their development needs because of the depth to which they go. This can be a good way of giving participants a 'felt sense' of what is required in new HR roles and creating a detailed development plan for individuals post HR transformation. The analysis of data across multiple development centres can provide information on the strengths and weaknesses of the HR function as a whole.

HOW TO CREATE THE BEST ASSESSMENT OR DEVELOPMENT CENTRES

PLAN

Like most endeavours, the success or failure of an assessment or development centre lies in the planning. It is crucial to spend time and thought with the sponsoring management on:

The need

Articulate in the clearest possible terms the business value to be obtained from this intervention.

Their commitment

Make sure there is a belief among stakeholders in using this approach and a commitment to using the results that will be produced, however surprising they may be.

Their intent and purpose

Work to develop clarity and transparency about the intent in building the centre. Surface any conflicting, dual or hidden agendas and resolve them. Get clear agreement on who will have access to what data and for what purposes it will be used. Also clarify the limits of the data's relevance.

DESIGN AND DEVELOP

Once the person responsible for designing and developing the centre has been fully briefed on the context, design work can begin to:

Analyse the job

Using a rigorous analysis process, develop a clear understanding of the role and the competencies/behaviours required for success. There is usually a long list to begin with that, on further analysis, can be reduced to a more manageable number of truly differentiating dimensions.

Design the centre

Design exercises, simulations and activities that will produce observable behaviour across all dimensions. Ensure each dimension is measured in multiple exercises. Make sure that exercises are discrete, so that performance in one does not automatically affect performance in another. Use the language, examples and culture of the business and ground all exercises and simulations in what really happens in the role. Double-check for any cultural or diversity implications in how behaviours are expected to emerge.

Design the aids and logistics

Prepare all paperwork to be used by assessors and others in running the centre (for example, behavioural checklists, evaluation forms, wash-up summary forms, role-playing 'scripts', exercise materials and timetable).

Train everyone

Thoroughly train all assessors and any role players required for the centre to a reliable standard of performance. Ensure they understand how each exercise will work, what it is measuring, what they must record and how, expectations of independence and the wash-up process. If role players are being used, ensure that they understand the simulations they are involved in, their role, their purpose and how much discretion they have in the moment.

Run a pilot

Wherever possible, run a pilot centre with an appropriate group of participants to check that everything works as it should and produces the desired outcomes.

Check quality regularly

Once the centres are running, periodically check the quality by attending and observing; reviewing outputs. Over time, measure the predictive accuracy of the centre by comparing assessments with what happens in the future.

Audit your centres comprehensively from time to time to measure the value they are delivering to the business.

All of these logical steps and how they fit together are shown in Figure 3.3.

PURE DEVELOPMENT CENTRES

Where organisations are committed to the incumbents in a role and want to help them create detailed development plans, we believe there is room for a different approach to development centres. The assessment aspects are removed altogether and the event is run as a true development centre in which the only objective is to foster skill development and no evaluative ratings are given.

Facilitators are more coaches than assessors. They still record, but rather than classifying and evaluating, they provide immediate feedback and encourage self-reflection. Participants carry the feedback forward through the centre, practising and reinforcing their learning as they go.

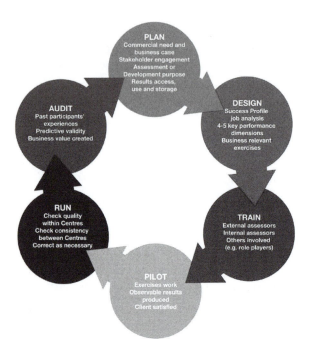

Figure 3.3   The planning cycle for assessment and development centres

Instead of an evaluative wash-up there is a participant-focused learning wash-up, leading to a development plan.

This approach could remove the discomfort many talented people feel when being judged or evaluated, make it clear this is an investment in the participants, remove doubt about hidden motives and position the event unequivocally at the development end of the spectrum.

JOIN IT UP

Clearly establish the links that do and do not exist between assessment or development centres and other HR processes. For example, show how results from the centre will feed into decisions about selection, promotion, succession planning, reward and training, and development. If decisions have been made that results will not influence certain processes, make that clear too.

CASE STUDY – DEVELOPMENT CENTRES FOR HRBPS

A major public sector department wanted to determine the skills and mindset of their 130 strong HRBP population. They were clear that this was to be a development activity giving participants a 'felt sense' of what was expected in the role in the future.

The department had a role profile and wished to align with the CIPD professional map. They therefore first created a 'Success Profile' to determine the success factors for the future role. This enabled them to create the development centre around fewer factors but to look at them more deeply. The centre was designed on pure development lines with:

- Coaches instead of assessors.

- A ratio of two participants to one coach.

- An atmosphere of support and fun.

- Exercises that reflected the demands in the role and the types of situations business partners could expect to face in the future.

- The creation of a development plan and buy in to the approach to achieving the development.

OUR TEN TOP TIPS FOR SUCCESS IN ASSESSMENT OR DEVELOPMENT CENTRES

1. Be very clear about the purpose and intent before starting design of an assessment or development centre.

2. State the use, storage, access and limits of relevance of the data.

3. Limit assessment dimensions to 4–5 true differentiators of success.

4. Measure dimensions in multiple exercises.

5. Have multiple assessors observe each individual.

6. Keep exercises discrete (they do not affect each other in any way).

7. Use simulations and activities that are directly relevant to the role.

8. Train assessors and any role players fully.

9. Complete all independent evaluations before wash-up begins.

10. Check quality regularly and audit periodically.

A successful talent management programme demands much more intervention, feedback and flexibility than most currently exhibit. Until these changes are made, companies will continue to be concerned about the quality and quantity of the internal HR talent that they have:

> *It can be very tempting for HR to follow fads and quick wins, talent management will not work unless the programme is robust and designed for the longer term.*

> *Head of HR, global luxury company*

SUMMARY

- Ensure the HR function has a comprehensive talent management process.

- Put in place flexible development options.

- Develop the whole of HR using common language and models.

- Use future focused training needs analysis to determine training needs.

- Use assessment or development centres to determine development needs.

- Execute your assessment or development centres using our ten top tips.

(4) Developing Your HR Function

For the last few years many organisations have undertaken HR transformation with a belief that getting the structure and technology right would deliver the value add to the business. When this did not result in an increase in the strategic impact HR was able to deliver, reskilling the HR team to deliver the promise of HR transformation became a major preoccupation of HRD.

Some of the most common problems that can arise when transforming HR are:

- Not enough development support is made available to HRBPs.

- HRBPs focus too much on the tactical issues and not enough on the strategic.

- Tension and hostility develops between the functions within HR.

- The HR team lacks any real feel of team identity or a common goal.

We have found that cross-functional development of the whole HR team is the most effective intervention at the point of change. There are many approaches to this but few of them have clear measures of success. However, there is clear evidence that HR development is crucial to success.

The CLC surveyed Chief Human Resources Officers (CHROs) at nearly 200 organisations across the world (CHRO Survey, CLC, 2006; Corporate Leadership Council Research). The survey sought to identify the critical skills needed for HR staff and identified a series of intensive methods to close critical skill gaps.

The CLC research correlated various strategies for building HR capability with HR's overall contribution to business performance. What emerged was the view that developing HR staff, rather than changing structure or implementing technology, was the most powerful path to increasing the function's effectiveness. The findings suggest that while technology and structural change do not drive performance as much as staff development, a baseline level of capability in these areas is needed to be effective. However, once this base line is met additional investment in the SSC, for example, will not make as much return as investment in development. The research showed that incremental investments in staff development led to more than three times the impact of investments in HR Information Service (HRIS) and twice the impact of changes to HR's structure.

Few organisations are leveraging this opportunity. Only 30 per cent of CHROs assess their organisations as effective in developing their HR staff in the context of a transformation to strategic HR.

Our own work with organisations would point to a growing trend towards putting in place development programmes for HR, but these still come behind new technology and restructuring the roles of the function. Development programmes are under utilised as an approach to making a significant change in the contribution of the HR function. We believe that HR development represents an under-leveraged opportunity in many organisations where the tendency is to invest more heavily in the technology than in the people.

In the context of an upgrading of the HR contribution to the business, it is particularly important for HR organisations to have staff with the business acumen and influencing skills needed to be strategic partners to the line.

Once the decision to invest in HR development has been made, it is also important to consider carefully how that investment is used. Of the many skill-building methods available, in our experience a few stand out as 'Power Methods' for building critical skills.

We recommend that organisations focus their investment on three high-impact skill-building methods:

- designing stretch HR roles that provide greater business exposure and personal challenge for staff;

- internal network building (for example, connecting people with skill strengths with colleagues who need to develop those skills);

- customised training.

Let us explore a little more about best practice in each of these methods:

STRETCH ROLES

It is well recognised in leadership development circles that giving talented managers exposure to stretch assignments or projects is the most effective way to develop their skills, test their potential and grow their maturity as leaders. The same holds true for HR professionals. Creating opportunities to move people around different HR roles and across HR and the business creates a deep understanding of the breadth and depth of the modern HR function and develops both technical skills and those needed to work with line clients and colleagues to influence change.

Our research into HR careers showed that leading a major change project successfully is a key requirement to getting the top HR role and at every stage of development different types of assignment can create new skills.

A well-structured and well-supported stretch assignment can be one of the most challenging and rewarding growth experiences people ever have. Care must be taken to get the stretch right – too much and it can overwhelm and failure will likely result, but too little and growth will not occur. Out at the scary edge but within fingertip reach is where to aim.

Job shadowing of HRBPs by SSC and CoE staff can be enlightening and useful. Job shadowing of line clients by HRBPs can be equally eye opening.

The best organisations plan in these stretch assignments alongside individual's career plans and are constantly on the lookout for projects and other opportunities to test their HR talent.

INTERNAL NETWORKING

HR people see themselves as poor at networking yet the most successful attribute their network as one of the key elements that has led to their success. Organisations that employ this method most effectively tend to:

- Actively encourage networking through setting up internal opportunities, such as conferences, off-sites and lunch and learn-type events.

- Use technology to help people get in contact and stay in contact. For example, one of our clients has set up an intranet portal that allow people to chat about HR issues, share best practice and access internal experts who could act as mentors to others.

- Reward, both through promotion and example, people who use and contribute to the sharing of knowledge through their network.

CUSTOMISED TRAINING

We see two areas where best practice reaps rewards. The most effective intervention is cross-functional development of the whole HR team at the point of change and covers the skills in technical HR topics, *what* HR need to be able to do to meet the business strategy as well as *how* HR need to work with the business and colleagues. This combination is essential for success. An imbalance leads to a technically knowledgeable HR function that does not have the skills to work with line clients to understand the business, influence and manage change.

The very nature of a shift to a transformed HR model creates the potential for fragmentation in the HR function. Silos can easily develop, as can toxic notions of first and second class citizenship between HRBPs and their colleagues in the SSCs and CoEs. We have found that by taking all parties through a common development process, they generate a common language and understanding of the value of the various roles. This directly countermands the tendency to separate and be at odds with one another as the new structure is established.

The second approach is to tailor the training to the exact needs of the organisation and to reflect their language, culture and the service model they are putting in place. This tailoring helps learning transfer back to the workplace as does incorporating methods to embed the learning.

We recommend setting up mechanisms to embed the learning over a substantial period of time. Through this it is possible to design ongoing cross-functional support networks and meeting opportunities, such as lunch and learn sessions and co-coaching pairs. Add to that the use of cross-functional action learning sets working on real-life projects between development modules and while investing in building the new skill sets, you also begin to build a new organisation that leverages and values its interdependencies.

As discussed previously, the return on investment case for focusing on skill development of HR seems clear. Making this an area of focus and an integral part of the HR transformation makes good business sense.

Consider how your own HR development activities match up against these 'power methods'. You may wish to ask yourself:

- Do you encourage and support all of these methods?

- Are the methods aligned to increase the value of the activities in each part?

- Do you reward people for their development activities, not just from a monetary perspective but with recognition?

DEVELOPING MORE THAN TECHNICAL SKILLS

Technical skills for HR may be the 'base case' but having a practical understanding of how to apply technical excellence in the business context is the key requirement.

Those HR people with the core and 'new' technical skills need the confidence to look at business needs and then practically apply their skills in, for example, change management in a way that meets the goals, culture and sophistication of the business. To develop this confidence and practical approach, people must have experience of working in change, OD and leadership projects in addition to the theoretical background. We have seen a few examples of development programmes that provide this systematically.

Best Practice – one development programme that achieves both the theoretical and practical elements of learning involves workshop-based learning focusing on the theory and best models in the area. This is supplemented by on-the-job application (preferably in the trainee's organisation) plus mentoring from an experienced practitioner.

As we have said, our research and experience show that it is important for HR team members to hold strong beliefs about their role in the business agenda. Without this sense of purpose and a belief that they can make a significant contribution to achieving the business goals, any development you give them will tend not to stick.

INTEGRATING HR DEVELOPMENT PROGRAMMES

Finally, ensure your development is integrated across the HR function. Creating a development framework with shared experiences across HR helps to create a culture of joint responsibility for the delivery of value added HR services.

We recommend an approach composed of three integrated development areas. This approach helps to develop an HR team that:

- has strong foundation skills – technical and process skills;

- is driven by the beliefs and mindset that our research tells us is the most successful for HR people to adopt;

- has clear experience of what the very best HR people do and how they approach working with the business and their colleagues.

CASE STUDY – BEST PRACTICE: CREATING AN HR CURRICULUM AND CAREER ROAD MAP

CLIENT PROFILE: A GLOBAL FAST-MOVING CONSUMER GOODS COMPANY

Our client's objective was to roll out a new HR structure along the lines of the Ulrich model. The HR transformation was staged over 3 years, starting in Europe and then rolling out through Eastern Europe, Asia and Latin America.

Orion Partners worked in partnership with the learning and development centre of expertise to design and deliver the global HR curriculum. This consisted of researching the skills needed in the new structure; including discussions with line managers and a cross section of HR professionals from each of the new functional areas – shared services, CoE and HRBPs.

The HR curriculum had two linked parts:

- The technical competence required by function and level. This matches the competencies associated with each functional role.

- The personal and business skills and mindset required to be successful in the new HR structure and to meet the HR vision of working in partnership with the business.

Part one provides technical skills workshops, e-learning and a toolkit. Additionally, in-house workshops run by CoEs to equip HRBPs and SSC staff with the necessary process understanding and knowledge in the CoE area of expertise. The toolkit was designed by Orion Partners to meet the needs for a common approach across the company that could be applied both within HR, for example, all HR people use the tools on project management when leading projects within the function and with clients. The toolkit also provided reassurance to line clients that a common methodology would be used across business units and geographies.

Part two of the HR curriculum was designed to provide HR-related skills that were crucial to the approach the organisation aspired to in working in partnership with the business. This is focused on:

- strategic skills

- managing client relationships

- skills in leading HR (leading HR is about taking a stand, having a point of view and being tough minded in order to achieve business goals).

This second part of the curriculum is delivered via workshops, and the tools and ideas are applied between workshops to real business issues. We are currently working with the company to introduce more self-directed learning tools in this area.

In addition, coaching is available to newly promoted staff at the point of transition. The coaching is provided to help people develop a strategic plan for their business unit or HR functional area and to apply the client/colleague management skills and personal skills to be successful.

As an extension of the HR curriculum Orion Partners are now working with regions that are not migrating to the new model for some time (Eastern Europe, Asia and Latin America) to provide pre-migration support, usually delivered through facilitated workshops, focused on the preparation of the HR team. This covers managing the transition with the line as well as the personal change and skills transformation necessary for individuals in the function.

Alongside the curriculum, the learning and development team have developed an HR 'passport'. The 'passport' is a description of the skills and experience needed to move across different functions within the new structure as well as the route to career progression up the hierarchy. This is used for career planning both by individuals and by the senior HR management when planning job rotation and development for individuals. The company has a history of managing job rotation centrally and so the 'passport' provides a means of discussing career options and measuring the success of the rotation plan in developing a sufficient number of individuals with the right experience to meet future roles and skills.

AT ORION PARTNERS WE USE A MODEL CALLED 'CREATING ONE' HR

The model overleaf summarises an approach to developing an integrated programme for HR as part of the transformation.

ONE HR IS MADE UP OF THE FOLLOWING ELEMENTS

CREATING MINDSET

Creating mindset describes the process that enables people to get a 'felt sense' of what the most successful practitioners do and some of the tools and techniques they use. It introduces:

- The different ways of working of the most successful practitioners.

- The beliefs and skills of the most successful practitioners.

- The interdependencies for success across the HR operating model for HRBPs, the SSC and CoE.

Participants gain a more complete idea of their areas of interest and needs for development across HR, as well as buy-in to their own ongoing development plan.

CREATING CAPABILITY

Within creating capability, any technical and process domain expertise requirements are addressed. This module combines a portfolio of skills modules with a series of supporting diagnostic toolkits.

CREATING SUCCESS

Working successfully as an HR leader focuses on:

- understanding and adopting the beliefs and skills that differentiate successful HR people;

- developing skills in managing, confidence, commitment and control to enhance self-belief and be more effective;

- developing tough mindedness to help participants challenge;

- identifying own biases to recognise when objectivity maybe compromised;

- recognising when independence is the key to success and how to maintain it.

Working successfully with the business and client focuses on:

- understanding and adopting the beliefs and skills relating to the business that differentiate success;

- knowing the business, developing strategy and conducting strategic conversations;

- understanding the business and matching its style;

- gaining buy-in to HR initiatives.

Working successfully with your HR colleagues focuses on:

- understanding and adopting the beliefs and skills that differentiate success when working with colleagues to ensure the business gets value from the whole HR function;

- contracting with colleagues in different parts of HR;

- identifying and managing different perspectives within the HR function.

MULTIPLE CHANNELS

In thinking about HR development, it is important to consider multiple delivery channels. Each has its uses and a balanced portfolio of all channels will achieve maximum effectiveness.

There are, on-the-job opportunities. A well-structured and well-supported stretch assignment can be one of the most challenging and rewarding growth experiences people ever have. Care must be taken to get the stretch right providing job shadowing for SSC and CoE with HRBPs can be enlightening and useful. Line client job shadowing by HRBPs can be equally eye opening.

There are formal development mechanisms that can be short and sweet or slowly rolled out over an extended time frame with action-learning opportunities positioned in-between:

- open programmes and workshops

- customised programmes and workshops

- executive HR coaching

- business degree courses

- distance learning courses.

Then there are the many forms of mentoring and networking that can be used:

- internal support networks

- support and challenge buddy pairs

- co-coaching pairs

- internal mentors

- external industry and professional networks

- 'lunch and learn' sessions.

Finally, there are the resource-based learning channels:

- reading materials and workbooks

- videos and film

- internet resources

- games and quizzes

- learning resource kits.

ENSURING DEVELOPMENT IS VALUED

If you want to look at how to improve staff engaging with development, you should start by considering how development is seen within the culture of your organisation.

Is it encouraged or is it seen as remedial, something that is only necessary if something is going wrong or someone is underachieving? If the latter, you will face a much more difficult task to get people engaged and receptive, this culture needs to be changed before anything will improve.

If, however, development is encouraged, there are tactics you can use to build on this and increase receptivity to development and engagement with it even further. These things should be built into the design of your event from the very beginning.

Perhaps the most important thing to do is to help people see the benefits to them personally of taking part in development. One reason why people do not engage is because they do not understand how it will be of use to them. In order to change this, you must get them to realise what is in it for them: What are the benefits? How will they be rewarded for participating? These questions need to be answered in a subtle way, but having compelling answers to these questions will help sell development to them.

When people understand that by taking part in the development, they are likely to be able to do their job better. Which in turn means their new skills will gain them recognition from colleagues. All this is likely to help them to enjoy their job more and they are more likely to be receptive to the process of development as a whole.

Additionally, there are a number of proven persuasive techniques that can be used to increase engagement. In his book, *Influence: Science and Practise*, social psychologist, Robert B. Cialdini outlines six 'weapons of influence'. At Orion Partners we have developed 'six tactics for influencing', which we have based on Cialdini's ideas but are relevant to development and including these in the design, publicity or content of your event can make all the difference to how receptive people are to it:

1. *Social proof* – people are more likely to take part in a development event or programme if other people they respect have already taken part. If the programme is for business partners, you can use the success of previous participants as an example to encourage others.

2. *Scarcity* – people want things that are hard to come by more than things that are easily available. If there are limited places on the development programme and it is difficult to get on to (or oversubscribed), they will be more likely to want to do it.

3. *Reciprocity* – people are more likely to do something for you if you have already done something for them and they therefore feel a debt or obligation. This would not always apply to development, but it may in some cases and you should always think about whether there is a key person that you can get to sign up for the development who owes you a favour that will in turn encourage other people to be receptive.

4. *Authority* – if those who run the development have a good reputation or the programme has been endorsed or sponsored by a member of senior management, it is more likely to be successful as it will seem more credible. It can therefore be a very good idea to ask a member of the senior management team to sponsor, champion or even speak at your development event or programme.

5. *Liking and likeness* – people have strong recognition for people in their network or who they feel are similar. If there are others attending the development programme or who have already attended, who they like or feel that they are like, they are more inclined to take part.

6. *Commitment and consistency* – if someone has agreed publicly, in front of others, that they will take part, they are more likely to stick to it as people like to be seen as consistent!

Building these six tactics into the positioning of the development, alongside using ongoing development and measurement techniques will increase receptivity to and engagement with development.

SUMMARY

Lack of skills has been identified as the single biggest barrier to successful HR transformation. To increase your organisation's chances of overcoming this barrier, follow our seven top tips:

1. Recognise that transformation of your HR function will challenge the existing skills of even your best people. It is not a reflection on the quality of your people – there are simply very different skills needed in all roles after transformation.

2. Conduct a training needs analysis or assessment/ development centre to understand where your people might struggle.

3. Invest as much as you can afford in developing the new skills.

4. Keep development activities as real and relevant to the challenges people are facing in their new roles as possible.

5. Create as many opportunities as you can to bring the whole of HR together across the new organisational boundaries.

6. Internal functional change is a great opportunity to prepare the next generation of HR leaders.

7. Provide blended learning solutions so that individuals can access the material they need in the format best suited to them.

(5) Career Management

USING THE HR STRUCTURE TO DEVELOP YOUR TEAM

In 2007 and 2008 Orion Partners undertook research (*Facing up to the Future*, available at www.orion-partners.com) into the impact that the transformation of HR had had on HR careers and career structures. Many of our clients had been telling us that the old career paths did not work anymore. We wanted to look at how careers were changing and how organisations were structuring career paths to develop talent in the future (see Figure 5.1).

The research primarily focused on how their careers had developed to date. Second, we asked the more senior HR people how they saw careers developing in the future, particularly in a transformed HR function. Most of our interviewees saw difficulties in developing HR careers going forward unless radically different actions are taken.

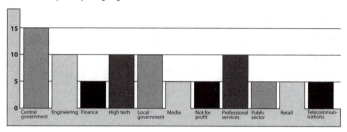

% Sectors of participating organisations

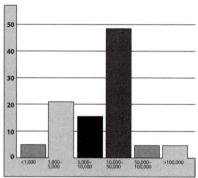

% Employee sizes of participating organisations

Figure 5.1   Facing up to the future research

In the 'old' HR structure there was a clear, well defined and proven career ladder. This meant that when people first entered the profession there was a distinct hierarchy, through which they could progress, learning along the way. In a transformed HR structure this natural career path is disappearing.

In the 'old world', people typically entered the profession in a junior generalist role. Here they could learn the technical aspects and HR policies associated with the job. As they developed and their responsibilities increased, they were given more complex projects, managed more important aspects of the HR calendar and dealt with more senior clients. Some moved to working in specialist areas, such as learning and development or compensation, but even if they stayed in a generalist role, they got the opportunity to gain some experience in specialist areas by working with their peers:

> *Because there used to be a hierarchy and a natural progression, people lower down the ladder had role models who were already successfully doing the next role up that they could learn from.*
>
> *HRD, luxury industry*

Under this system, while they were learning the technical aspects of the role, they were also gaining valuable skills in dealing with clients, influencing and working with increased complexity before taking on full responsibility for outcomes. There was a clear line of sight that showed HR professionals what they had to do next to progress their careers. While the 'old' system had its flaws, it did in the main demonstrate a clear career progression picture so that people could identify the skills and competencies that they would need to move up the ladder. The line of sight's disintegration is further complicated by HR's split into three distinct areas that, in the main, require different skill sets.

The rise of the SSC and CoE are filtering staff earlier than ever into specialist roles. This has had a direct impact on the ability of mid-career managers to move across the function, as they do not have the depth of knowledge required. In addition, the very nature of CoE and SSC management roles isolates them as specialists from the HR functions and businesses they support.

Specialism in process management in the SSC or technical expertise in CoEs, brings real advantages in allowing the HR function to develop new capabilities. For some this has been a refreshing change, allowing them to pursue specialist careers more easily. However, for many, this prevents them moving easily into new management roles to gain a broad overview of the function at the mid-level.

Our research identified that:

- It is possible to make structured moves to cover a number of specialisms at an early career level. This becomes increasingly difficult as staff progress in their careers.

- Organisations that have embarked on transformation, but have not deliberately addressed the issue of building generalist experience, have had to seek mid- to senior-level talent from outside to fill HRBP roles.

- Frequently mid-career HR professionals have had to find a generalist role to consolidate progress in the CoE and SSC and take the next career step.

- The level of specialism inherent to CoE roles for mid-career professionals can very quickly leave them isolated from the organisations they support:

> *Broad operational HR experience is crucial to both understand the business context for your actions and to be taken seriously in future senior roles ... you can only get that by living it. I have really seen people struggle to influence without it.*
>
> *Associate HRD, advertising and media services group*

GROWING YOUR HR POPULATION'S SKILLS AND EXPERIENCE

We have already mentioned the anxiety that exists about developing a cadre of HR people. There is no doubt this is a new challenge for the function and one that requires more flexibility, discipline and innovation than may have been needed in the past.

THE NEW GLASS CEILING

Something to be aware of is that transformed HR structures frequently create a large gap between SSCs, CoEs and HRBP roles. There are now few, if any roles, which will develop the next generation of HRBPs. Our latest research consistently found that those in early career roles with ambitions to develop are struggling to move on from the SSC roles and are hitting a glass ceiling; clearly a major de-motivator.

The research identified that:

- Some of the key skills required for HRBP's relationship management and business understanding are not developed in the SSC.

- The emphasis on the HRBP job itself is distracting people at earlier career levels from taking the roles that will get them into those posts – no other role seems to matter.

- SSC roles can prevent early career HR professionals from getting a good business understanding and developing a sense of 'what will work' in the organisation.

- Organisations are losing candidates at early career points as they seek generalist experience in smaller organisations with more traditional HR functions to allow them to break out of the SSC.

Our senior level participants who reflected on how early 'coalface' experience was critical to moving on identified an example of this. This was in most cases through employee relations roles. Surprisingly these roles were not valued for the HR technical knowledge provided, but because they built understanding of the business while establishing credibility and empathy with business managers. All of these, in more sophisticated forms, are key skills for an HRBP. This in itself is a very interesting point; an aspect of HR that appears to be undervalued generally is a very useful source of experience for developing skills and mindset for the transformed HR function:

> *The HR employee relations role is about really knowing the business and its people, it is about understanding the shop floor and making an impact in that environment. My training ground for that was dealing with conflict between people as part of my first role as a graduate trainee. We are not creating enough opportunities for our people to learn that now.*
>
> *HRD, professional services firm*

The research examined the impact this is having on those moving out of their first roles. HR recruiters, Digby Morgan, provided their observations:

There is a shortage of good business candidates with a depth and breadth of HR knowledge and who are good communicators and relationship builders. Their most successful candidates are those who have built a broad base of skills before specialising, these candidates tend to come from smaller organisations.

In smaller companies, while the Business Partner, Shared Service and Centre of Expertise model may not be in place, candidates have been exposed to a broader range of HR activity. Candidates in larger organisations have typically had more structured early careers, but do not often show the breadth of skills needed to move on, with many coming from narrow shared service backgrounds. These candidates are finding that they have to move organisations to obtain the breadth they need to move on in their HR careers.

Director, Digby Morgan

Few organisations have carefully thought through how to develop key HRBP skills as part of their implementation of new HR services. However, as we have seen, many are now rethinking HR structures and development programmes as a result of pressure to build internal HR talent.

In summary, our research found that a structure that includes a SSC, CoE and HRBPs has a significant impact on the roles within HR. Many organisations are struggling to map out the new career paths that are emerging. Many are also struggling to equip the next generation of HR professionals with the skills and experience they need to develop their careers to their full potential.

The transformed HR model offers a wide variety of routes to success. The model below shows some of those routes in a typical transformed HR structure (see Figure 5.2).

To structure career development you need to define all career paths clearly and help people to understand the routes that are open to them. These routes may include:

- Moving through increasingly senior HR roles in one area, for example, in a CoE.

- Developing a deep specialism in a CoE or an area of the SSC.

- Becoming a specialist in operations and customer relations in the SSC.

Potential career paths in the 'new' HR model

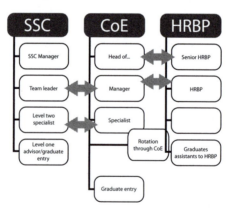

An example of different career paths in HR

Figure 5.2   HR career paths

- Following a career that is partially in HR and partially in other areas of the organisation. For example, the SSC's customer service manager will have the skills to run customer service centres in other disciplines.

- Rotating through the different HR disciplines and gaining business acumen to become a fully rounded generalist with career options in any of the functional areas of HR – SSC, CoE or HRBPs.

Providing different career paths demands:

- An open dialogue with staff to determine their interests and talents.

- A clear description of the skills, beliefs and experience required to progress along a chosen path.

- A reward structure that takes into account the different career options. This would need to include rewards for people managers as well as rewards for those who choose to take a specialist route.

It is important to educate the HR team during the early days of transition to the new structure. In most companies it is also essential to educate the organisation and to market your HR team's skills. This will open up career paths outside HR, particularly for operational specialists and HRBPs who can make a contribution in the business generally.

BEST PRACTICE: CAREER PASSPORTS

These are very useful. They describe the experience and skills an HR person needs to succeed or to move through the different career routes and describe the minimum requirements for the key roles in the organisation. For example:

- skills and competencies for the role;

- previous experience;

- attitude and mindset;

- possible assignments that contribute to achieving the requirements;

- a description of any failings or issues that would block progress.

The best of these 'passports' is a clear guide while also being flexible enough to open up opportunities rather than close them down. For example, experience of working with other cultures may be a role requirement. This could be achieved through working in virtual teams, undertaking charity work outside the organisation, past experience as a student or while growing up rather than just through company assignments abroad.

MANAGING CAREERS

In our experience the best approach to career management includes a thorough review of the current and desired state for success. The process includes diagnostic review, mapping and assessment, career development and measurement and evaluation.

DIAGNOSTIC REVIEW

You identify and understand the career path challenges and issues you are facing, and the implications for the function together with the options you might take. These might cover anything from simply increasing internal rotation, shadowing and mentoring, to a wholesale rethink of approaches to skill development and career progression.

MAPPING AND ASSESSMENT

You create a career path roadmap that shows the possible routes to various roles and the skills and experience needed to make each move. You may also choose to assess the capability of your people so that you and they understand where they currently are and what they need to add to progress successfully.

CAREER DEVELOPMENT

You create an HR curriculum or similar consisting of workshops, action learning and other development methods: this links to your careers roadmap. The most sophisticated often include online access to learning materials via a web portal and give the HR team multiple means of learning and managing their own careers.

MEASUREMENT AND EVALUATION

Having defined success, you ensure you have systems in place to track and monitor your progress towards your HR career management goals (see Figure 5.3).

BEST PRACTICE: CREATING AN HR CAREER MAP

Case study – client profile: the organisation is one of the biggest financial services firms in the world.

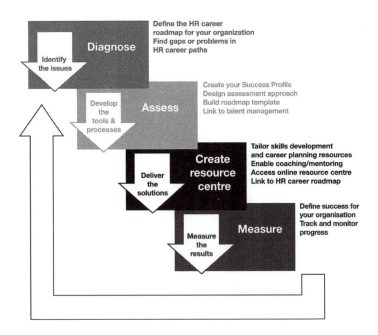

Figure 5.3   The process for creating a career structure

Orion Partners worked with the Head of HR Professional Development to create an HR map for career development. The goal was to create a virtual resource centre that:

> *Clearly defined the role of HR in creating value in the business; this was about* what *HR was expected to do; the processes and tools to be used, and* how *HR would work with the business – the style and 'philosophy' they adopt.*

Directing HR professionals to the potential roots for career development; it defined competencies, both technical and personal, and the experience that would count towards career progression across the group. This included job posting and descriptions of typical roles with details of skills and experience required, as well as descriptions of the different businesses within the group and the style and culture of each major business.

Provided details of the development tools and resources available; some of this was about rationalising the number of workshop-based courses, aligning the messages in workshops-based development. For example, creating a common language and models, and reducing the number of suppliers used. The details about workshops also enabled potential participants to gain insight into the views of colleagues on the benefits of the development options. This area also provided self-directed learning through e-learning, reading, self-managed learning groups where people could come together to share experience and the application of learning in the business.

Created an HR community, with forums for discussing business issues; getting input from colleagues on the use of tools; and the creation of a team of volunteer mentors who were experts in a particular HR process or tool. These mentors provide guidance to colleagues who are using the process for the first time or have a particularly difficult project to manage.

The resource centre is delivered via a web portal and is accessed by over 2,000 HR professionals across the organisation.

JOB ROTATION

Job rotation is important for HR people who want a career of increasing seniority in the hierarchy, such as HRBPs and those who want a managerial career. We believe it is essential to understand the workings of the whole function. Designing routes that allow for this and having the mechanism to facilitate the moves is a requirement for success. This demands that HR participates fully in the talent process and has:

- a clear assessment of talent;

- the ability to assess people's beliefs about how HR roles are carried out and the criteria for success;

- the provision of career guidance to help direct people to the best career path for them;

- assignment planning;

- enough resource to enable rotation without damaging service levels.

There is also a need to eliminate status and kudos differences between operational and strategic roles. We have written elsewhere of the necessity of giving equal reward and status to these roles (*Personnel Today*, article 'Trade Secrets – making it as a Business Partner', October 2006). However, we still hear stories about organisations that are struggling with this. One client moving to the transformed HR model found that their best people were not in their SSC. People had been reluctant to apply for these openings, seeing the equivalent level role in the CoE or as an HRBP as higher status. It took the organisation time and money to reassign people and much persuasion was needed to convince some to make the move. Starting your transformation by embedding a clear understanding that all centres are essential and provide opportunities for progression is a key to long-term success.

Best practice – one of the examples of best practice structuring we have seen is the creation of two or three extra headcount positions reserved for recognised talent. The people assigned to these roles are rotated through the different HR functions and key positions, such as an SSC customer service role or a CoE consulting role. These roles can also be used for assigning individuals to special projects. This works best in projects that touch all aspects of HR. Elsewhere the additional headcount has been used to create executive assistant roles to HRBPs. This is a great way for someone to gain an insight into the world of HRBPs prior to having the skills to actually do the job.

CLEARLY DEFINE ROLES

Confusion about the role HR plays in the new structure. Developing HR people means that you need to clearly define the role they play. Having clear descriptions and working practices that define the boundaries between roles is also essential. Development on and/or facilitated sessions on how the HR team works together in the business context accelerates performance and the transition to the new HR structure. Many companies have paid insufficient attention to this aspect.

Job descriptions are helpful, but are not the only answer. Providing a model of how a role adds value to the business can help to put it in context. In Figure 5.4 we describe examples of these models showing how value is added to the business.

This model illustrates the context within which HRBPs operate. Overall focus is on achieving the business strategy and goals. Success is achieved through a combination of local HR plans and agendas, coupled with corporate-wide strategic initiatives.

The HR calendar is an ongoing reality for the HRBPs. There are two areas of focus. One is the day-to-day needs of the business and, the other, furthering strategic HR initiatives. So, for example, the way in which the regular compensation review is handled may be tweaked to emphasise a strategic goal in a particular area of the business.

Figure 5.4   The roles and context for HRBPs

The HRBPs play several roles in the business. Each role may be more or less important depending on the HR/business agenda. It is rare for the HRBP to spend extended periods in one role. Rather, they are likely to engage in the roles simultaneously to achieve a key objective, such as coaching a senior manager through an issue while also acting as a consultant to help a part of the business move forward with a goal.

The ability to act as both an external and internal facing function is the key for success for CoE people. They must monitor and understand the potential impact of external trends and have the skills to translate these into policy and strategy (see Figure 5.5). At the same time, it is essential they monitor and analyse business trends and can adapt policy and process accordingly. The important areas to track are:

- business goals

- shifting emphasis in executing the strategy

- competitor's actions.

They are also the function that must reconcile competing demands related to HR policy across business units.

The four drivers of success for SSC managers that we have identified (see Figure 5.6) sit alongside their responsibility for seeking improvements in processing, delivering a great customer experience and deep data analysis to identify the root cause of problems. Having the ability to identify patterns of success and failure enables them to apply these areas of focus to the places where the greatest value will be added.

MODEL OF THE STRATEGIC CONTRIBUTION OF THE CENTRE OF EXPERTISE

SKILLS
Making Connections, Asking Strategic Questions
Provider of external expertise, Question assumptions, Challenge
Create solutions

| THE BUSINESS STRATEGY

HR Strategy | UNDERSTANDING THE RELEVANCE OF EXTERNAL TRENDS
Competitor
Economic
Political
Regulatory | STRATEGIC CONTRIBUTION
HR Policy
HR Corporate initiatives
Trend analysis
Raising the questions for debate
Reconciling needs of business units |

The roles and context for Centre of expertise staff

Figure 5.5   Strategic contribution of CoE specialists and managers

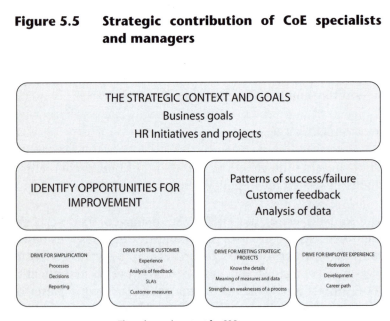

The roles and context for SSC managers

Figure 5.6   Drivers of success for the SSC manager

VARIETY IS IMPORTANT

We have seen a number of companies that have managed this process well. One client employed a very successful rotation programme. This consisted of looking at how people were working in their current role and putting together a thorough description of what they were doing, the level they were working to and the skills that they had.

The next step was to create an in-depth description of the skills an individual needed to develop at various levels and then to identify all the key roles within the business that might provide experience to develop those missing skills. For example, if the employee needs experience of running budgets, they could be rotated into an assignment that included budget and/or profit and loss responsibility.

However, although a rotation programme can work very well, it must not be the only string in the development bow. HR needs to use a combination of approaches, such as mentoring, coaching and training. By using a variety of development approaches it accommodates the differences in how people learn and respond to different types of input. The different approaches that a programme might include are:

- job rotation

- stretch assignments

- experience in different parts of the business or different parts of HR

- projects

- mentoring

- coaching

- training and development events

- reading

- self-directed development via web-based learning

- working with buddies and more experienced colleagues.

DEVELOPING YOUNG TALENT

Giving the new HR recruits (graduate or similar) early exposure across the function is the best approach for developing the skills of young talent. Entry level programmes that rotate participants around the function work best, provided that real work assignments with responsibility are given early on.

BEST PRACTICE: ENTRY LEVEL CAREER DEVELOPMENT PROGRAMME

One of the best programmes we have seen demonstrated the following features for encouraging participation from across the company:

- The programme involved assignments to various parts of the company both within and outside HR. Participants with a preference for HR would have to do at least one assignment of their four outside the function.

- Participants had a senior level mentor who gave career advice and followed their success through the programme.

- The programme co-ordinator provided counselling to participants, monitored the quality of assignments and participants' progress.

- Internal competition for participants was encouraged. So assignments were typically well thought through.

- Programme participants formed alumni that acted as a useful network after the programme.

- Formal training was provided in core business skills, such as finance and self-presentation.

Some of the benefits of this type of structured programme are:

- Participants develop an understanding of the business and the different functions that make it up.

- They gain exposure to senior management (through the mentoring programme) early on in their career.

- They develop a network of peers (through the alumni group) who are useful contacts across the company but have also been shown to help stem turnover at crucial career point's after the first 2 years. In one company we saw this alumni group continue through to participants being 10 to 15 years into their career.

- They receive crucial feedback and coaching (from the co-ordinator) on career choices and their need for skills and exposure to different part of the organisation.

An HR Graduate Trainee, from a Global engineering company said:

> *Early exposure to the breadth of the HR function is a core part of our company's approach. I'm spending three to four months on each project area as part of my graduate training programme. The variation is what attracted me to the role and it is building my skills in all areas of HR. How to communicate with the business is the biggest thing I'm learning.*

A rotation scheme is built into the career plan of anyone identified as a potential future business partner at a global mobile telecommunications company:

> *I've worked in several teams across the SSC, from resourcing through to ER advisory roles. Now I've been placed in a secondment to a Business Partner role with a view to becoming an HRBP within six months.*

> HR adviser

HOW TO ACQUIRE BUSINESS SKILLS THROUGH CAREER MANAGEMENT

To what extent do HR people in strategic roles need to have spent time in line roles and roles outside of the HR function?

We see a trend toward businesses recruiting from outside the HR function in order to bring in business and strategic skills. While both of these methods can be useful, neither is a guarantee of success nor necessary, in our view, in creating a team of people with strategic skills. Our experience and research suggests that capable, intelligent people are able to develop business and strategic skills if they hold the right beliefs. That is if they believe in being commercial, are interested in the business and in their own continued development.

One way to create opportunities for HR people is to be more forceful in marketing the skills HR gives people. This can be done through the talent process as well as informal channels, such as participation in cross-functional projects.

Below we have summarised the results of our '*Facing up to the Future*' research on how senior HR people seem to have gained benefit from assignments.

BEST PRACTICE: DEVELOPING BUSINESS SKILLS

Following promotion to her first HR management role, leading an expatriate support team in a global oil company's CoE, the Head of HR at a large-scale public sector employer actively sought her next move outside of HR.

After sitting down with her mentor and mapping out the experiences she needed to make her next move, a need for commercial and greater line management experience was high on the list of priorities. The best place to find that was by moving out of the CoE and HR altogether. By maintaining strong links back to HR, she felt that she would be able to return later.

After a successful period as an area retail manager, she returned to a more senior generalist HR role working directly with the line, with a real depth of business knowledge and fresh ideas. Her instinctive recognition of the business drivers and metrics that mattered allowed her to step confidently into this HR generalist role.

LEADING CHANGE IS THE ONLY WAY TO THE TOP

Most successful HR leaders are not just great HR professionals, but have led significant change in the business. This experience has given them the opportunity to move into the most senior roles. At the entry point to senior management, individuals given the opportunity to lead key projects and programmes, appear to benefit significantly in a number of ways. Such projects invariably bring them closer to the business and provide HR leaders with a clear platform to drive the business forward, with enhanced credibility.

Orion Partner's research identified that skills gained by HR professionals who led change programmes include:

- the ability to put strategic thinking into practice

- planning, project and programme management skills

- people leadership experience

- increased knowledge of the business

- international/ overseas exposure

- experience of running a business operation

- commercial and financial acumen

- change management

- broadened networks

- risk management and decision making

- application of the full breadth of HR know-how

- lean process management techniques

- performance management and metrics.

Such activities are not simply confined to large-scale restructure or HR information systems implementation, but include setting up and leading other function's service centres, mergers and acquisitions (M&A) integration, offshoring and leading a business operation outside of HR.

From the survey of our leadership level research participants (see Figure 5.7):

- 71 per cent had led major change and 64 per cent experienced a direct benefit to their career;

- 36 per cent achieved promotion within 1 year;

- 21 per cent achieved promotion within 2 years.

Where they had been involved but not led such projects, individuals did not achieve a direct career benefit.

The types of change initiative were varied and can be seen overleaf. The research showed that to gain full benefit, individuals need to have successfully led such change programmes with both visible and tangible benefit to the business.

Type of change project participated in by HR leaders

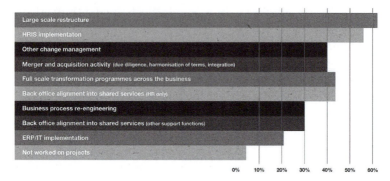

**Figure 5.7   Types of change project within which HR
leaders have participated**

To date, most organisations have not taken a formal approach
to equipping HR professionals when they are thrust into such
programmes. In the main there has been a 'sink or swim'
approach. Individuals made their own way by:

- 'Learning on the job' and using opportunities earlier in
  their career to watch or shadow others.

- Building their networks, attending thought leadership
  events and working with professional services consultancies
  to develop a broad skill set to support their work.

- Undertaking specific learning in aspects of programme
  or operational management, or within a related business
  field. This is an area that needs more attention and to be
  given recognition as a key element in the HR career path.
  It must be actively integrated in the personal development
  of future HR leaders.

Career examples from leaders in the 'Facing up to the Future' study:

- IIRD, Telecommunications services provider – after a fast track career in the RAF within engineering and training, he built his career largely by leading programmes including large-scale training programmes with significant reskilling and behaviour change. The major step came with implementing and running HR services centres at a major UK bank and high profile public body. He is now focusing on large-scale business transformation within his current organisation.

- Senior HRBP, global transport engineering company. She built her career on a series of overseas rotations in Europe, USA and Asia. Here she worked on and led, large-scale programmes, including the setting up of CoE, undertaking M&A integration and significant scale restructuring.

- Head of HR capability, major government department – moved into a leadership role in the public sector. After supporting performance and development work, he was given early exposure to help set up a new HR function in a UK-wide department. He was soon promoted to head up the reward centre of excellence, which saw him lead a large-scale workforce restructure, before heading HR services and moving to his current role on the leadership team.

BEST PRACTICE: CAREER PLANNING AND ROTATIONS

One of our clients, a major oil company, has mandatory placements for high potential HR people in non-HR areas. In the retail sector we see many HR graduate programmes that include a rotation in a non-HR area and non-HR track graduates rotating through HR. If well designed, this type of programme ensures a deep understanding of different aspects of the business while treating all participants as equal in their development.

The transformed model does not translate to a lack of career paths for HR people, but it does require people to create a more intentional career path. Before implementing the model, HRDs need to think about creating career paths for the future and build them into the HR structure's design.

Your functional structure and the experience you give people is an effective way of developing your HR team.

The combined practices found across the organisations interviewed in 'Facing up to the Future' form a model for successful HR development (see Figure 5.8). Implementing this model in your organisation will require you to tailor it to your learning culture and career management approaches. However, conscious application will produce your organisation's HR talent of the future.

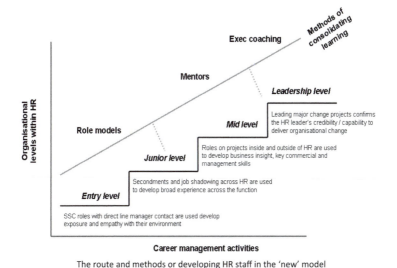

The route and methods or developing HR staff in the 'new' model

Figure 5.8   The HR talent ladder

All the organisations participating in the research had evolved their approaches over time and we are able to draw some key lessons from their experience of what has worked for them:

• *Doing nothing is not an option* – the fracturing of the traditional HR organisation means that only a proactive approach to HR development will produce the right HR talent to meet your organisation's needs.

• *Take a holistic approach* – individual HR job design must take account of the roles that act as stepping stones and be integrated into your overall HR career management framework.

- *Integrate your approach with non-HR career management processes* – HR processes must integrate with the wider organisational processes for career management, if they are to offer the right range of non-HR opportunities (for example, leading business projects).

- *Prioritise key roles to have the greatest impact* – focus on managing the careers of your mid-level roles at the start, these are the hardest ones to get right and are the visible face of the HR function to most managers.

- *If HR is not seen as a strategic partner, start with that first* – the senior management of your business need to see HR as a strategic partner if HR staff are to take the high profile roles needed to develop talent.

- *Look for the right behaviours and potential* – finding the entry level staff with the right behaviours, potential and 'fit' is more important than chartered institute of personnel development qualifications.

- *Real investment of time and money is required to achieve success* – wasting talent in an HR function is as great a sin as wasting it in the business. Real investment is required to produce results.

- *Ensure your definition of 'talent' is broad* – when looking at defining the requirements for HR talent in your organisation, avoid being too narrow. It should cover behaviours, values and technical HR skills.

- *Clearly signpost the key roles* – the HR team at all levels need to know which are the key roles that provide a stepping stone on their career path through their 'passports'; role models, formal communications, awards and talent programmes all have a role to play.

- *Pick your role models and mentors from beyond HR* – they are essential to support HR talent development, but they should be drawn from both inside and outside the function.

SUMMARY

There are a number of common areas that successful organisations are focusing on. These include:

- A clearly articulated description of the experience, skills and knowledge a future HRBP needs and the types of roles that will best provide that experience.

- Talent management processes that describe the career path and stepping stones to moving across and higher in the HR department.

- The identification of separate career paths for the different parts of HR. Such as a path for those who wish to stay in shared services.

- The hiring of staff with different attitudes and skill sets. Such as when recruiting for the SSC, ensuring that there are some positions that require the skills and beliefs needed to be a senior HRBP or CoE specialist down the line.

- Finding opportunities for some SSC and CoE staff to be assigned to work on projects and assignments that involve direct contact with HRBPs. In this way, the 'natural hierarchy' can on some level be recreated as staff work alongside the HRBPs and take responsibility working in line roles or at least on business projects.

- Building structures with clear links between all parts of HR – working out the potential early career moves and focusing on the skills needed to make each move.

- Using roles, such as case work advisers in HR, and expanding the scope of roles in contact centres to support talented early career staff to build business exposure.

- Ensuring that the change projects the most senior HR professionals lead, are high profile and deliver significant, tangible business benefits.

- Setting up early career project and secondment opportunities to reinforce the career progression opportunities built into the new structure.

- Using role models and more formal communications to clearly signpost future career paths after leaving entry level roles.

⑥ Attracting the Right Talent

We are always seeking a formula for proving development's value and making it worth the investment. Here we look at some ideas for helping you achieve that. One of the dilemmas of choosing to spend money on training and development is the lack of tangible evidence of a return for your investment. Will the behaviour and success of your HR team significantly improve to match the money you have spent? There are some important considerations that will help ensure that this happens.

The first is ensuring that your development programme is aligned with the purpose and beliefs of your HR team. Most training and development focuses on the skills and competencies of the trainee. However, if we look at models of change like the logical levels model overleaf, we see that people (or organisations, who are just groups of people after all) will not change if the suggested shift is inconsistent with the purpose and beliefs they hold about their success and reason for doing their job the way they do.

THE LOGICAL MODEL

The model is split into six levels – each looking at different factors that need to be right for successful change to happen. Starting with the bottom one, these levels cover:

SPIRITUAL FACTORS

These link to a person's view of the larger system to which they belong. This is about for whom, or for what, a particular action is taken.

IDENTITY FACTORS

These relate to people's sense of their role within the organisation's mission and who the person or organisation perceives itself to be.

BELIEFS AND VALUES

These look at the attitudes people have that may move them towards success or away from it. These attitudes provide the motivation to act and persevere. They relate to why people or organisations do what they do.

CAPABILITIES AND MINDSETS

These are the mental maps, plans and strategies that lead to success. They relate to how success will be achieved.

BEHAVIOURAL FACTORS

These cover the specific actions or steps required to achieve success or simply what must be done to be successful.

ENVIRONMENTAL FACTORS

These relate to the external opportunities or constraints that must be recognised and acted upon. It involves understanding where and when successful change occurs.

Many initiatives undertaken by individuals or organisations focus on the higher levels – the environmental and behavioural factors and capabilities around change – but do not pay enough attention to the more intangible areas covered in the lower levels. Without making sure that people's beliefs and values, identity and sense of purpose are also prepared for change, the initiative is probably doomed to failure – something we will all recognise from experience.

We like this model because it works in practice, not just on paper. Our experience also backs up Dilts' theory (*Visionary Leadership Skills*, Robert Dilts, Meta Publications or see www.nlpu.com) that change will only occur if people and organisations actually identify with the goals that a change is trying to achieve and make the achievement of these goals something of personal importance.

Engendering a sense of purpose and tailoring development to this, while also ensuring the programme addresses the team's mindset (purpose and beliefs) as well as their skills, is a key component of getting a return on your investment.

To successfully develop and embed skills and beliefs the old adage of 'what's in it for me' must be addressed. Many HR people see the change to the new structure as more of the same. They also tend to be a tad arrogant about their own development. It is their job, after all, to develop others and admitting they need some too does not sit easily. We have found that the context in which development is framed is important. It is not helpful to frame your initiative as remedial or to fill the 'gaps' that your team has if they are to be successful in the future. It is also often not true, unless we are describing a pure skills gap, such as a legal change or a complete lack of exposure to OD, for example.

Framing your needs analysis as looking for 'the difference that makes a difference' in the highest performers and directing your development to achieve these aspects has inherent advantages:

- it is a more positive message;

- it acknowledges the skills and success members of the team have already had;

- it builds on, rather than hopes to stop, current behaviour;

- it helps the best hone their skills and develop greater flexibility – all aspects of high performance;

- it focuses your development on achieving mastery or high performance rather than building remedial skills.

CREATE A LEARNING ENVIRONMENT

Creating a learning environment is an important element in developing the HR team. We wanted to share some of the things we have seen work well.

Clearly, job rotation and learning through participation on projects is a key element, as are tailored development workshops. To make development really stick, we find you also need to move learning closer to the job to ensure it becomes part of the role rather than an add-on that happens at special events or at certain times of the year.

Additionally many companies are turning to the use of web-enabled technology to aid them in creating a development framework along with multiple learning methods and resources. As well as the 'passport'-type approach mentioned previously, the best of these include:

- job rotation;

- e-learning programmes, especially useful for technical skills;

- tailored resources, such as links to websites and reading material;

- the use of in-house coaching and mentoring;

- the use of external coaching and mentoring;

- creating HR networks either with or without the use of area champions/subject experts;

- short updates and learning 'pills' that reinforce subject matter from workshops or update on business and technical information;

- 'lunch and learn' events that incorporate networking and encourage the exchange of best practice across the organisation.

BEST PRACTICE: EXTERNAL MENTORS

One client created a network of mentors within its competitors. The HR person received mentoring from a senior person with industry experience while also learning about the approach of the competition. Reciprocal arrangements were part of the programme, as were agreements on confidentiality. This programme quickly broadened participants experience; increased their networks and widened their approach and thinking:

> There is a lot of good practice and innovative ideas around, but integration is the key to a really effective development programme. Ensuring the different strands work together to create more than the sum of their parts is where real value is created. This is enhanced further when reward systems, both monetary and promotional, reinforce the development focus.

One of the common issues with HR development is that the focus rests on the actual training course or development event rather than on the ongoing development of the team. We believe that the event itself is simply a catalyst for change, but often through lack of time or clear direction, many HR development programmes are not capitalised in day-to-day practice.

When planning an HR development event, it is easy to focus solely on what will happen during the training or workshop and forget about what happens next, when people return to work. If application in the workplace has not been sufficiently considered, or is simply an afterthought, it is more difficult to get people to practically apply what they have experienced. It is essential, therefore, to design the transfer of learning into the development event rather than think about it as an add-on or afterthought.

ENCOURAGE LEARNING THAT STICKS

There are many techniques that can be used to encourage learning that sticks. These do not differ from what you would design into a development programme for any other part of the business, but for some reason we do not always see this with HR programmes. The ideas below can be considered a reminder and some examples of best practice.

One of the most effective ways of helping development stick is to make it as real as possible to the participant's day-to-day work. For example, instead of fictitious case studies, *work on real examples from your business*. This will make the transfer of learning to the workplace easier. Rather than focusing on theory, *include lots of practical tools and techniques* that you know will be applicable immediately in everyday work situations.

Recognising that development continues after the event and designing this into the programme from the start works best. *Consider setting up a buddy or coaching scheme* at the event for continuation afterwards. The buddy approach involves pairing two people, with similar development issues, during the event so they can support one another's learning on their return to work. Alternatively, with internal coaching or co-coaching schemes, peers either coach one another or someone in the organisation with coaching skills can take on the coaching role. Again, these individuals should be introduced during the event. If there is no one in your organisation with coaching skills, you could investigate using external coaches.

You can also try giving each person from the event one of the recommended books to read, insert a comment card inside the back cover and encourage them to note the most relevant or insightful sections and then pass it on to someone they think might find it useful (whether that person attended the development session or not). This will help to extend the learning into the practical environment. One of our clients did this with very positive results. The reputations of the most useful books spread around the organisation. Soon there was a waiting list, not just for reading, but also to peruse colleagues' comments and how they applied the ideas in the business.

You can also use a company intranet to set up a virtual learning community. After a training event, individuals can access and continue to use materials, websites, books and any other tools used. A chat forum will encourage and facilitate the exchange of ideas to help to ensure that the learning continues to be discussed and applied.

Using experts as mentors is another option. Where individuals in your business are given the responsibility of keeping up-to-date in a particular area they excel in and then mentoring others who want to improve their skills in that area. This can also work well by being set up during a development event, identifying those with strengths in specific areas and pairing them with those who are less strong in those areas.

BEST PRACTICE: THE YELLOW BRICK ROAD

This company believed that they had most of the resources they needed internally to develop their HR team. To make these resources accessible, they created 'the yellow brick road', a document that described the skills and experience necessary for success in HR roles and gave it to experts from within and external to the company who could help. People across the HR team volunteered to be subject or skills experts. This required them to keep their knowledge and thinking up-to-date and to act as a coach to staff wishing to improve skills in their area. So, for example, the expert on performance management was responsible for the following:

- keeping up-to-date on the latest trends and best practice on performance management;

- making this available through a website;

- creating learning events;

- coaching or mentoring colleagues;

- acting as an expert consultant when new performance management processes were being introduced or modified.

This was replicated for all the key technical and skills areas, such as relationship management.

To cover areas like 'knowing the business', key questions were produced that directed people to the knowledge they should have and where to find it, together with the names of volunteers around the business who were happy to explain, for example, the technicalities of the management information system or the features of a particular product.

Action learning is effective. These facilitated groups come together periodically to share learning and to be challenged on how they are applying it in the workplace. As well as going over material covered at past development events, incremental training content can be rolled out at these sessions.

BEST PRACTICE: ONGOING LEARNING

The client had run an HR development workshop and followed it up with 'lunch and learn' sessions to achieve two objectives. The first was to reinforce the learning from the workshops. This was achieved by asking participants to present case studies of how they had applied the learning and the results they had achieved in the business from using the tools and ideas presented in the workshops. They extended the learning from the workshops by covering topics of interest in more depth. Second, the meetings were used as an opportunity for the HR team to network and discuss topics of interest and identify areas where they could help each other out. This resulted in a greater return on the investment from the initial workshops and a broader and more long-term application of the ideas. It also helps to keep the contacts made in the workshop and interest in learning alive. Finally, the sessions created their own momentum with participants suggesting topics for future meetings and participating in running the 'lunch and learn' events.

BUILD A COMMUNITY

The aim of all these ideas is to build a learning community of event attendees – an alumni network who can continue to learn together and extend that knowledge and learning throughout the workplace. The advantage is that the learning is not forgotten and can be adapted and applied as new issues come up. The development event becomes not an end in itself, but a catalyst for long-term change.

People are naturally attracted to the ways of learning that suit them best and this differs by individual. It is therefore important that a range of techniques are used to give people access to learning in the way that suits them best. If these are built into the course design from the beginning, there is more chance that the learning will stick.

Encouraging participants to engage with the ongoing learning activities involves them in holistic learning and is important for the transfer and embedding of new skills into the day-to-day business. If the learning and development department or an external consultancy is leading all the learning, it is likely to run out of steam more quickly.

These types of programmes work best when participants see the benefit of the ongoing learning and provide the energy themselves to keep it going.

The techniques used to maintain ongoing learning will change as the needs of the group develop. The needs on day one will not be the same after six months. The ongoing learning strategy needs to develop with them, as does the way you measure effectiveness. If you have incorporated this from the planning stage, you should be able to adapt.

It is also worth remembering that any development event needs to have a finite lifespan. It can not continue indefinitely as the dynamics and needs of any group involved will change over time. So while it is important to make sure your development is more than just an event, give it a finite life – it is unrealistic to think that it will go on forever.

Measurement is an important way of providing pay back for those people that get more involved. From the very beginning, ask yourself how you will measure effectiveness. First, to help you assess the success, work out what data you can collect and how easy it will be to gather. Ensure that you incorporate a practical data collection method at the planning stage and make one person responsible for ensuring it happens. Practicality is important; it is no good if it costs more to measure than the actual learning event did.

In order to collect the right information, you will need to think about the participants' objectives as well as the HR management team and business stakeholders. So it is important to be mindful of what they will all consider to be relevant and make sure your measurement fits.

There are many techniques for collecting data, both qualitative and quantitative, for example, if the aim of your event was to make HRBP more strategic, you could carry out 360° feedback to gather information about how strategic they were before and repeat the exercise six months later, noting any differences in the response.

Alternatively, if your event was aimed at developing SSC customer relations skills, quantitative data that is probably already routinely gathered can be used. For example, you can compare customer satisfaction rates over a period of time.

Finally, try to create a culture within HR that encourages learning and where those who learn are recognised and respected. Some companies have a culture where it is frowned upon to take staff out for training or it is seen as 'skiving', but this must not be the case if you want development to stick. This attitude is less likely to prevail in workplaces where learning is ongoing and the results show.

MEASURING RESULTS

There are several theories and levels of measurement. Ultimately the most important measure is that you have a cadre of talent to deliver the HR agenda; add value to the business; keep that talent in the company; and fill positions as they become open. However, you may also want to gain the opinion of your key stakeholders. One of the methods we recommend is the 180° feedback survey. The way the survey works is described below.

A series of searching interviews is conducted with key stakeholders on the HR team's performance to obtain qualitative and quantitative feedback to help the team understand both how well they are performing and which elements of their offering are most valued by the stakeholders.

We have a standard questionnaire of 27 questions covering recruitment, compensation, employee relations, learning and development, and performance management, with additional questions on quality of service and future priorities. This can be fully customised to the needs of our client with additions, deletions and changes as required.

Stakeholders are asked to evaluate the team's performance as strong, adequate or weak against each element and to say whether this element is critical, important or not important. These answers provide the quantitative feedback. Qualitative feedback is then obtained by probing for examples to illustrate the reasons for their rating and, if appropriate, what they would need to see to improve their score. Interviews are conducted by telephone and last between 30 and 45 minutes each.

We aggregate and analyse all responses and compile a non-attributable feedback report. Results are usually fed back in a 2-hour long group workshop with the whole team, during which we ensure the results are fully understood, provide flavour and tone, answer questions and help the team decide their priorities as a result of the feedback. We extend this meeting to half a day if the team wish to begin immediately to prioritise actions and to form a plan.

The output from the stakeholder survey would form the bases of the HR development and adjustments to tactics and execution, as well as set the base-line for future evaluation of the HR team's performance.

SUMMARY

To help ensure that both the HR function and the business achieve a return on investment in HR development, you should consider:

1. Ensuring that your development programme is aligned with HR's purpose and beliefs.

2. Not just focusing on skills and competencies, consider the implications of the logical levels model in your design.

3. Framing your development in the correct context for your people.

4. Creating a learning environment with many strings to the bow above and beyond classroom or web-based learning.

5. Making your learning stick by making it relevant to the 'real' business.

6. Creating follow-ups to learning events with participant support through mentors or co-coaching schemes.

7. Building a community that encourages and recognises ongoing learning.

8. Pragmatically measuring the effectiveness of development programmes.

(7) Achieving a Return from Your Development Investment

The scarcity of talent and skills presents a compelling need for HR to attract and then retain individuals that fit their HR profile. In the CLC research (*Defining Critical Skills of HR Staff*), CHRO assessed their organisations effectiveness at recruiting skilled staff externally. An average of 40 per cent rated themselves effective at this approach.

But what type of talent are you searching for? First, you need to decide if you are looking for HR talent across the board or seeking people with the specific attributes to work in the SSC, CoE or as HRBPs. It is, however, also important to recognise that there are some commonalities across HR; a number of core skills needed, such as business acumen, innovation, metrics and client management.

Most HR departments have well-defined competencies and a clear idea of what experience and qualifications they require of their staff. Yet they tell us they still find it difficult to differentiate good candidates from the best candidates.

Qualifications do not always tell you what you need to know. A candidate with near perfect qualifications does not always do the job well. While someone with unremarkable qualifications could turn out to be the highly effective person you are looking for. Our research found that the difference that makes a difference can be attributed to the candidate's values and beliefs not their qualifications and experience.

I believe that the way to find a candidate with potential is to look beyond their competencies, to their personal values and this belief is backed up by our research at Orion Partners, which identifies a common set of values among the best HRBPs. These values drive their success, whatever environment they work in.

We are beginning to see a pattern in the values of the best HR people. We also have evidence that these values are common across the best HR people but may be independent of the values of their function or the company in which they work, for example, HR people holding values that are not shared especially by a transactional HR function.

So, if there is a set of core values that you should look for at interview, which can define a great HR person, regardless of qualifications and to a greater extent, regardless of working environment, what are they and once you know what they are, how do you recognise them?

UNDERSTANDING THE CORE VALUES

The first is to be commercial. We found, that regardless of the company, the most successful HR professionals saw their role as a fully commercial role and this meant that they took a far more strategic approach to their work. It also means they only do what they can see adds recognisable value to the business goals.

A strategic approach also means taking a 'longer' term, 'big picture' approach to HR and you need to look for people who can prove they can think beyond the day-to-day. The ethos of your new employee must match the company to a degree, but it must also match what you are looking to add to the HR team and these are not necessarily the same thing – think about your company's corporate goals and objectives and consider how they fit into your HR department's goals and objectives, and then consider how your employees should fit into both.

The best HRBPs are also results oriented. This means not just following HR best practice. Some HR people can be more concerned with process than with results and this is not always going to produce benefits for the business. Candidates should be able to demonstrate personable credibility. Strong people are usually recognised for the times they make a difference. The more this happens, the more others will seek out their opinion when decisions need to be made. This vitality results in those people with personable credibility having courage in their convictions, meaning they stand up for their views and push back when they know something is not the right thing to do. The more that people are seen as credible, the more they will be able to make a commercial, results driven difference.

And finally, they have a desire to learn. Wanting to constantly improve what they offer is the best way a person can ensure that their methods and tactics are kept fresh; if they are never quite satisfied then they keep pushing to know more and improve their performance.

IDENTIFYING THESE QUALITIES AND VALUES WHEN RECRUITING

So, now you know what the values look like, how do you identify them? Someone can tell you their beliefs, but can they actually prove them during interviews? How do they articulate those beliefs? Interviewers can structure the selection to seek evidence of the drivers that determine how the HR person performs their role. They need to demonstrate their motivation through use of examples that show their beliefs in action. In this way, interviewers are able to identify the values behind those motivations.

You also need to determine what those beliefs and values means to you and how you expect someone to translate that into behaviour. If someone says 'I would like to make a tangible difference in a business' this might be music to your ears, but does this mean the same thing to you as it does to them? How do they want to make a difference? How do they make judgements and decisions? Ask them to give explanations or examples of their beliefs so you can make sure you understand how that belief translates into behaviour.

You may also want to discover what they consider acceptable and unacceptable when working with clients. Internal clients can be challenging, especially when dealing with issues, such as confidentiality and ethical issues – how does your potential employee deal with them? Again real examples tell the story not hypothetical responses.

TACTICS AND PRACTICALITIES

The final thing you need when recruiting for qualities and values are practical methods to achieve this. Methods can include standard ones, such as using structured interviews that simply have a stronger focus on identifying beliefs and requesting presentations that focus on qualities and values. You may also consider using a belief questionnaire, a system developed especially for this situation by Orion Partners and you may wish to provide your interviewee with case studies of interesting or difficult situations and ask how they would deal with them. If you look for these qualities and values, your HR people will naturally become more commercial and therefore, more productive.

A senior HR leader from the *'Face up to the Future'* research describes the role qualifications have played in her:

> *I have gained my CIPD qualification, an MBA and become an NLP coach ... these were the entry level qualifications in my move up the career path they got my foot on the next rung of the ladder but I found that the qualifications did not accelerate my career you also need to get lucky and find that person who can give support and direction, an informal coach to guide your learning.*
>
> *Vice President HR Transformation,*
> *global transport engineering company*

121

One method for ensuring you are seeking the attributes which really make the most difference is to adopt a method like our 'Success Profile'. We have devised a methodology that reveals the four or five key differentiating factors between average and exceptional performance in any given role. We call this the 'Success Profile'.

SETTING THE CONTEXT

We start by asking your HR leaders what has made the company and HR function successful to date, what their vision is for the future and what it will take to get there. If there is any confusion within the leadership group, we help build a consistent view.

GATHERING THE DATA

We help to identify your highest performers; those who are already performing in a way that meets your future goals. We interview each of them in depth, using a structured format that elicits information about instances when they have been exceptionally successful in their role and times when they have been less successful.

We drill down into detail about their experiences at five levels:

1. *When and where* – the circumstantial environment in which the event occurred.

2. *What* – the actions they took; what they did.

3. *How* – the capabilities they drew on; how they decided on the actions.

4. *Why* – the beliefs and values that drove their decisions and led to their actions.

5. *Who* – their sense of identity and purpose in the situation; who they are in their role.

This approach builds on techniques used in developing competency frameworks, but produces a richer picture of the full conditions that generate success by exploring deeper dimensions; the how, why and who.

THE ANALYSIS

We analyse the data by searching for the consistent patterns between individuals across the population and conduct a two-way feedback sessions. Participants tend to discover things they were not previously aware of about themselves and their successes.

THE 'SUCCESS PROFILE'

We compare and contrast your HR context with an individual's profile to build the company 'Success Profile'; a clear description of the key distinguishing factors that set the best people apart from the rest. We can also use our database to benchmark HR staff against HR professionals in other firms.

IDENTIFYING THESE QUALITIES AND VALUES WHEN RECRUITING

Now you know what the values look like, how do you identify them? Someone can tell you about their beliefs, but can they prove them during interview? How do they articulate those beliefs? Recruiters can structure the selection process to seek the right data. The best way to do this is to simulate the work environment through an assessment centre.

EXAMPLE FROM OUR HRBP BELIEFS QUESTIONNAIRE

We have found that traditional selection processes will not always pick up on the latent talent of candidates. However, selecting on candidates beliefs and values can identify the right people for further development.

The specific HR technical skills can be taught as part of the induction.

ATTRACTING MORE SENIOR LEVEL HIRES

Many believe that hiring in experienced non-HR managers with strategic and operational skills can help transform HR. While this may well bring skills into the profession; there is also a danger that it will erode the important technical skills that HR brings to the business. Parachuting in external expertise may represent another example of HR's lack of confidence and self-belief.

However, non-HR hires can bring some useful skills and the necessary technical skills can form part of the induction process. This is the mistake we have seen in some businesses. Hires from the business are put into HRBP roles without the benefit of a full induction and technical skills building. When non-HR hires come into the function there needs to be a concerted effort to induct them so that their expertise can be melded with those needed in their HR role. Some of the best approaches we have seen give mature hires a structured induction into HR, both from a technical and positioning viewpoint. The worst example we have seen is based on an assumption that business skills are all that is needed and the technical HR skills can be ignored. The consequence of this have been clearly seen in the recent economic down turn. Business partners who came into HR from different functions were suddenly at a loss on how to advise the business on the technicalities of downsizing and similar programmes. The result being a lack of performance and an erosion of the very confidence and skills they were hired for.

An example of best practice on inducting non-HR hires to business partner roles is given below.

Best practice: senior induction. One of the best induction approaches for non-HR senior hires we have seen was in a company that hired HRBPs internally. These people were experienced in the business, but lacked technical HR skills and client relationship focus. The company hired each one a coach who worked with them through their personal transition and building client skills. The coaches were all ex-HR, so were also able to advise and recommend approaches to filling the gaps on the technical side. Alongside their coach, each person was assigned a technical champion, an experienced HR person in the business known for their expertise in, for example, legal or benefits matters. This person gave initial training and then acted as a mentor for future issues and advice.

INDUCTION OF YOUNG TALENT

In the transformed HR structures, early exposure across the function is the best approach for young talent. Entry level programmes that rotate participants around the function work best, provided that real work assignments with responsibility are given early on.

Best practice: Entry level career development programme. One of the best programmes we have seen demonstrated the following features for encouraging participation from across the company. The programme involved:

- Assignments to various parts of the company both within and outside HR. Participants with a preference for HR would have to do at least one assignment of their four outside the function.

- Participants had a senior level mentor who gave career advice and followed their success through the programme.

- The programme co-ordinator provided counselling to participants, monitored the quality of assignments and participant's progress.

- Internal competition for participants was encouraged. So assignments were typically well thought through.

- Programme participants formed alumni that acted as a useful network after the programme.

Formal training was provided in core business skills, such as finance and self-presentation.

SUMMARY

When hiring in HR talent:

- Create a clear specification of the success factors. Focus on the attributes which will make the most difference and recruit against them.

- Use selection methods which will test the candidates against the success attributes not just their past experience but their beliefs also.

- Assessment centres can be a useful tool for selection.

- When hiring in people without pervious HR experience ensure their induction gives the context and technical skills to achieve success in the role.

- When hiring inexperienced HR candidates create a rotation programme that gives them broad experience across the different elements of the function.

(8) Conclusion

The new world of HR is about more than structural change and a new technology approach. The change simply creates a framework. It is how the framework is interpreted for your specific organisation that facilitates the capability and drive to deliver what the new HRIS system and business centric HR structure promise. At the end of the day, whether your transformation delivers added value to the business will depend on the capability of your HR team.

That takes careful planning and this should be built into the HR change programme right from the beginning. You are asking your people to operate in an environment that places very different demands on them. Recognising this and carrying out a skills audit early on to identify who best fits where in the new model is essential. Once the right people are in the right place, it is vital that they are upskilled for their new roles and career paths for the new world are created. Any gaps should also be identified early on and an internal (from outside of HR)/external hiring process initiated that will bring in the right sorts of people with the right skills, values and behaviours for your organisation.

In our work with a number of organisations in equipping the HR function with the skills and knowledge to deliver effectively, we have come to understand the following ten top lessons learnt:

1. Organisations will have outstanding examples of people who live and breathe the required behaviours and provide excellent role models for others to emulate. Time spent understanding how these in-house role models get things done pays great dividends in quickly understanding what works in a particular culture.

2. Keep it simple. There are normally four or five key competencies that distinguish the best from the mediocre. Identify what really matters in your organisation and focus on embedding a few simple but effective skills in the majority.

3. Do not over-engineer your training solutions to cover all options and eventualities, concentrate on the areas identified as key and those of biggest impact.

4. Blended training works. Use a mix of written material, classroom and scenario-based learning (with relevant real life settings/examples) to make your training meaningful and memorable. Back this up with a mentor/co-coaching programme to ensure that training continues to pay dividends back in the business.

5. Good e-learning is expensive to develop and of limited impact when driving behavioural change. It is effective in the delivery of basic knowledge delivery, but it requires significant investment to make it memorable and enjoyable.

6. Capture the voice of the HR people. People are typically very honest about their technical skill and values failings. The best people to help you identify key needs are the HR people themselves.

7. Ensure you have a robust talent management process that is integrated into the system for the whole organisation.

8. Map career paths and the route to different career options and identify separate career paths for the different parts of HR. Such as a path for those who wish to stay in shared services.

9. The hiring of staff with different attitudes and skill sets. Such as when recruiting for the SSC, ensuring that there are some positions that require the skills and beliefs needed to be a senior HRBP or CoE specialist down the line.

10. Training evaluation should occur at three points: (1) by the participant at the end of the course; (2) by the participant's line manager three months after the intervention; and (3) finally as part of a 360° evaluation 12 months after the programme (though frequently time and resources may limit the evaluation option to two out of three of these possibilities).

Orion Partners

Orion Partners are leading independent advisers in HR Transformation. Established in 2002, we have led and managed HR Transformation programmes for over 30 blue chip clients and our client base covers leading organisations in both private and public sectors.

We help organisations to succeed in their HR transformation by enabling them to:

- Clarify and define HR's strategy and role relative to the business.

- Decide on the most suitable operating model for HR, including the option of shared services or outsourcing.

- Select and implement the right technology solutions.

- Assess and select the right people.

- Develop the skills and mindset to succeed.

- Make the transformation happen on the ground.

Our unique focus is the whole range of HR transformation activities. We pride ourselves on the independence and practical nature of our advice and our focus on identifying and capturing the benefits in our design and implementation. We have skills and expertise in scoping, design and change management of the transition.

We have a have a broad base of functional, industry and global experience. Together with deep knowledge of HR and what makes it work successfully. We undertake regular research in the HR field including our unique studies on the difference that makes a difference in HR Business partners and HR Leaders.

If you would like to find out more, please visit www.orion-partners.com or call us on +44 (0) 207 993 4699.

GOWER HR TRANSFORMATION SERIES

This series of short books explores the key issues and challenges facing business leaders and HR professionals running their people management processes better. With these challenges comes the requirement of the HR function to transform, but the key question is to what and how?

The purpose of this series is to provide a blend of conceptual frameworks and practical advice based on real-life case studies. The authors have extensive experience in all elements of HR Transformation (having between them held roles as HR Directors and Senior Business Managers across a range of blue chip industries and been senior advisors in consultancies) and have consistently come up against the challenges of what is the ideal new HR model, what is the value of HR, what is the role of the HRBP and how can they be developed?

Whilst the guides all contain a mix of theories and conceptual models these are principally used to provide the books with solid frameworks. The books are pragmatic, hands-on guides that will assist readers in identifying what the business is required to do at each stage of the transformation process and what the likely options are that should be considered. The style is entertaining and real and will assist readers to think through both the role of the business and transformation project team members.

If you have found this book useful you may be interested in other titles from Gower

Six Sigma in HR Transformation:
Achieving Excellence in Service Delivery
Mircea Albeanu and Ian Hunter with Jo Radford
Paperback: 978-0-566-09164-3
e-book: 978-0-566-09165-0

Going Global:
Managing the HR Function Across Countries and Cultures
Cat Rickard, Jodi Baker and Yonca Tiknaz Crew
Paperback: 978-0-566-08823-0
e-book: 978-0-7546-8134-2

Managing HR Transformation:
Realising the New HR Function
Ian Hunter, Jane Saunders, Allan Boroughs, Simon Constance,
Tracey Bendrien and Nicola Swan
Paperback: 978-0-566-08828-5
e-book: 978-0-7546-8166-3

Visit **www.gowerpublishing.com/hrtransformation** and

- search the entire catalogue of Gower books in print
- order titles online at 10% discount
- take advantage of special offers
- sign up for our monthly e-mail update service
- download free sample chapters from all recent titles
- download or order our catalogue